The ScreamBed Chronicles

The last days of playas & other insecure men

VIORI
PUBLISHING

Viori Publishing
PO Box 5283
Atlanta, GA.31107
http://ARIsphere.com
You may contact Ari Meier at Viori
Publishing at ari@vioripublishing.com

The ScreamBed Chronicles: The last days of playas and other insecure men.

ISBN: 978-0-9887805-2-1
PRINTED IN THE UNITED STATES OF AMERICA

Readers Comments:

"AMAZING! This book is a real page turner that gives an entertaining account and perspective on love, life, and relationships".
LaToya Gardner, Indianapolis, IN

"I am a fan of The Screambed Chronicles. I love this book, from the personal essay testimonials to the blow-your-mind erotic poetry; TSC hits all the right notes. Trust me when I say that you will read this book from cover to cover as soon as you pick it up because you never know what the author is going to say next". **Arvell Poe, Actor, Vinings, GA**

"This book shows the personal growth of a "player" evolving into a real man. It is sprinkled with poetry and lyrics and the essays are informative and delightful. I finished this book within a day because I could not put it down. Every woman and man should read this."
Violette Meier, Author of Angel Crush, The First Chronicle of Zayashariya: OUT OF NIGHT & Violette Ardor: A Volume of Poetry & This Sickness We Call Love: Poems of Love, Lust & Lamentation-Atlanta, GA

Ari Meier

Dedications

I dedicate this book to all of the women and men that are in loving relationships.

Contents

Contents

Special thanks

To my mom, Margaret Rose, thank you for your guidance, love, and nurturing and for birthing more girls than boys; this helped cultivate my respect for women. I love you. I thank my dad James Perry, you taught me how a real man provides for his family and I know that you are whispering great 'making money' tips from the other side while I sleep. Love you. I thank my children, Kiera, Arman, Aura, Xoe, Zahyir and Ruah for bringing more love, patience, and their teachings into my life. I love you.

To my sisters Evadne and Sheri, I learned how to be a woman liberator from growing up with you women, with me looking out for you and your best interests. I love you.

To the love of my life Violette, thank you for your great ideas, patience, and support. I love you googol times infinite. I thank my late grandmother, Violet Evans, my late aunts Sophia and Sarah. I saw firsthand, what makes a strong woman by your examples. Though you all were on different ends of the personality scale, you shared the commonality of strength with a mixture of feistiness, intelligence, and genuine love of people. Love you.

I thank my late grandfather, William Evans, who was my model and inspiration for how to treat women. I can still remember the days of you "shaking and

Special thanks

baking" chicken while sharing your knowledge about any and everything. Love you. I thank my Uncles Benny, Wink, and late uncle Brainerd. You all inspired me to be who I am, and you showed me that real men cook, clean and actively raise children. Love you all. I thank my uncle, Yemi, who continues to inspire, motivate, and elevate my consciousness in new directions, especially when it comes to women.

Last, but not least, I thank the women who allowed me to tell their stories in the essay, "When the Girls Go Out". Though many of us have gone our separate ways, I am reminded of your invaluable input when women read the essay and they tell me that this is their favorite.

Preface

A few years back, I realized that sometime back, I did some fucked up shit. No, not some crazy criminal stuff, but you can call some of it crimes of the heart. I was an emotional pimp, a major liar and mind gamer. Thinking back on all this, I knew that I needed to respect women more. Though, I did respect women on a basic level, I started feeling bad about the wasted time and busted hearts, that were caused by my lower level of respect and genuine concern for their emotional state.

What was really going on inside of me? I soon realized that my game playing was about me being insecure with my place in those relationships. I avoided completely handing my heart over to most of my girlfriends as I was afraid of getting hurt. I presented myself as the ultimate mystery man, a romantic slickster supreme. Nevertheless, I knew the truth, as my inside self really screamed 'nervous mess', and geek-boy. I only fooled others.

I decided to put some words down on paper, but I did not want to write a typical relationship book. I wanted to do something simple, something that could be read quickly. I wanted readers to get into my head and feel my emotional sickness masqarading as 'sowing my wild oats'. The book had to expose some of my stories, as embarrassing and heart breaking as they were. The good thing was, I had already written essays dealing with relationships and about treating women better, this were good. This book is made up of short essays and poetry that can be shocking, erotic and obscene (sometimes all in the same essay), but they are honest.

This book is like my apology to the women and girls (of course, my younger days!) that I hurt both consciously and unconsciously because of my playa ways. In addition, I respect and love everybody and it is not my intention to hurt anyone or make anyone feel less than a respectable human. However, I don't care for any dudes that may hate this (if your actions are being exposed); and this book is NOT aimed at the many good brothas that are in great relationships. This is for the girls and women that are in crazy relationships who need a little light so that they can find the door and get the hell on.

Brotha 2 Brotha

Brotha 2 brotha
i've been meaning 2 tell u
about how u treat her
she'll do anything 4 u
when u show your true heart
the words come from high
brotha make the start
the special feelings u can't deny
brotha if u feel u got her
don't stretch her feelings no more
if u betray her trust and love
she'll just walk out the door
brotha 2 brotha
brotha 2 brotha
she's been trying 2 say some words
u say she's stupid and silly
or don't know nothing at all

The ScreamBed Chronicles

with these kinds of words
it's a wonder
u have a love at all
brotha if u feel u got her
don't stretch her feelings no more
if u betray her trust and love
she'll just walk out the door
brotha 2 brotha
brotha treat her like a queen
brotha don't b so mean
cause brotha she's your baby
she's a part of u
(and she's thinking of u)
brotha, brotha treat her like a queen
brotha don't be so mean
brotha (because she's your baby
and she's a part of u
she's thinking of u)

Song, "Brotha 2 Brotha"

Brotha 2 Brotha

"When brothas wake up to the love, essence and vast potential of the sista, that's when the black family will flourish" – Ari Meier

Heard on an Atlanta subway train: first brotha: "Man these bitches ain't shit, that's why I have many of 'em." Brotha # 2 "Yeah, and this ho who I have a baby from, was talking about me giving her some money to buy some diapers, I told her; I don't have nuth'n for ya." Of course, they talked loud enough for the sistas on the train to hear.

Brothas, we need to treat our sistas better! We need to respect them more and express some of our innermost feelings to

The ScreamBed Chronicles

them. I am sure that some men may think that I am whipped or lame for saying this. That's okay. To those men, I say that you're lame, because you're the one that keeps undermining the foundation of your potential happiness, well-being, and wealth by being shit stupid. We must keep in mind that every time we diss a sista, we are dissing someone's mother, sister, grandmother, or aunt. Still don't care. What if it's your mother, sista, grandmother or aunt?

Life for much of us could be much healthier and more fulfilling if we just treat sistas or anybody for that matter, the way we want to be treated. Much pain and chaos could be eliminated if we would just see the God in our 'baby mama' instead of just seeing a sista who's getting child support, or seeing a strong woman who demands basic respect, instead of seeing a bitch.

Brothas with the sista, you have an energy so great and powerful that if she's allowed to be herself, free of a super jealous, hating, abusive man, or in a relationship without excessive drama, she has the potential to help lift up the family unit to greater heights.

Brotha 2 Brotha

How did we get to this point in many of our relationships? There are many theories out there regarding the why's, what's and who's, one of which is involving the slavery era practice of separating the African families, thus helping to create future generations of 'family breaking' black males.

We could have academic discussions on slavery's 'legacy' (which has been discussed as nauseum) or we could discuss ways to deal with the realities of today's issues, which is there are too many black fathers leaving their families behind.

Historical accounts of most indigenous people show that women were held in high regard as there were many feminine festivals and celebrations (many that are the source of today's Judeo-Christian Holidays). Women held high positions in tribal life and were highly respected because of their spiritual powers. While men may be physically stronger than most women, the feminine spiritual energy, when focused, is just as strong and relevant as physical strength. It can heal, it can protect, and it can destroy!

Knowing this, it's apparent why manyEuropean religious authorities feared, prosecuted, and eventually killed hundreds of thousands of mostly European women in the name of stamping out 'the Old Religion'

The ScreamBed Chronicles

or witchcraft. Women around the world knew how to channel this same spiritual energy. They primarily used the energy to strengthen their bond with the Creator, to help heal others and to connect with the unseen or spiritual world.

Yes, brothas, sistas can be this heavy in the spirit. But you need to be a more positive part of her life and one way you can do that is to get to know yourself and be honest with yourself. While you may know a little about the history with slavery, with its family destroying design, that's the past and this is the present. Stop making excuses for why you are not getting shit done or why you can't treat your woman right or better. It's time to 'boss up' or start handling your business in the present. Now is the time to evaluate yourself and get to know your true self. After doing that, it's time to be honest with yourself by exposing the bullshit in your own head, open the doors of the secret closets within your personality and mind. There are many ways to open the deepest doors in the closets of your mind. Some people do what is called a vision quest or visioning, which most indigenous people around the world practice.

Brotha 2 Brotha

It involves going alone into the woods for a certain amount of time (ranging from a day to a week or more). While in the woods, you may face your fears: fear of insects, spiders, wild animals, the dark, and of being alone. You eventually learn to trust and develop a stronger faith in nature and the Great Spirit. You pray, meditate, and see the connectedness of everything in the universe. Of course, this is an oversimplification of the vision quest; any good Native American-written books on this ritual should be consulted.

Some people do a regression, which involves being hypnotized and while under hypnosis, the subconscious mind is awakened. Before you cringe in fear at the word 'hypnosis', hear me out. Many times, while undergoing a regression, most people can remember long forgotten current life and/or past life events, events that may have triggered their current habits, fears, or behaviors.

According to many spiritual and religious studies, most people in the world believe in reincarnation.

The ScreamBed Chronicles

Even if you are in the minority who does not believe, it will not necessarily stop you from experiencing a past life or earlier life memory while under hypnosis.

Also, most people undergoing this type of therapy usually find it amazingly effective in dealing with phobias, traumas, the "why me" or "bad things always happen to me" situations and bad habits in their present life. There are many regression therapists around the world, and you would not have to change your religion to use the services of one.

Below are some simple steps that could be taken to get to know yourself. Acknowledgement is the first stage. Acknowledge that you have three parts: spirit, body, and mind. For much of humanity's existence, we have focused more on the physical and not as strong a focus on the spiritual.

Sure, people do spiritually inclined things such as going to church, meditating

Brotha 2 Brotha

and praying, but many of us are blind followers without a clue as to what being in the spirit is all about. There is nothing physical about it-no churches, no temples, no meditative or prayer positions to adhere to. You are simply acknowledging your connection to the Great Spirit. There is no certain way to meditate or pray, just start small. Devote as little time that it takes to make the call to God. Quiet your mind. When you get restless or if your mind starts wandering, break the connection. You may devote a few seconds or a few hours each day.

But be consistent with it. After a while of making the connection and acknowledging God, now it's time for the hardest part, which is exposing your conscious, mind to what's in your subconscious.

This could be the most negative aspects about you. Ask God to enlighten you to your innermost negativities and just chill out and listen. Sometimes this may seem to take forever, due to our distorted views of God and the messages that we receive from God.

The brothas who are in relationships may see the negative part of themselves played out in their wife or girlfriend. It could have been going on all along, only the brotha was not aware because it is in much of man's nature to be reactionary, instead of being

The ScreamBed Chronicles

spiritually in tune. When your woman is showing a negative side of herself to you, instead of reacting as if it is being directed to you, it may be a part of you that you are being shown to learn about so that YOU can change for the better.

During, the self-revealing phase, you will see the different aspects of you in your friends, their relationships, in books, newspaper articles and dreams. The key to all of this is your sincerity in wanting to change for the better. After the big self-revelation, go back to your spiritual telephone and ask the Great Spirit for guidance about changing the negative traits to positive traits. The key again to this is the intensity of your sincerity in wanting to change for the better.

When you can conquer your personal demons, that is when your wife or girlfriend's real and/ or perceived negative behavior may diminish. Remember, for the most part, that your woman's disposition may be as good (or bad) as yours is. You attract to yourself, what you are at the deepest level. Many people feel that they are good on the inside and have attracted bad people for no reason. Usually this is just a reflection of themselves, on the deepest levels being shown outward or something to help them transcend the heavy negative energy and flourish.

Brotha 2 Brotha

The mind is like a mansion with many rooms, and each room has many closets and each closet have many storage boxes. If you think that your mansion is clean because you can't see some of the trash and junk that you've piled in the closets, or you think your closets are clean because the storage boxes hide the mental junk, then you are fooling only others but not yourself. When learning about yourself, get deep into the rooms, the closets, and finally the storage boxes of your mind before you can absolutely utter the words: "I'm a good person stuck with a bad person and I don't know why".

The last part of the 'getting to know you series' is maintaining what you've learned. Just as a body builder must maintain his or her physique, by weightlifting and doing other exercises, you must maintain your newfound spiritual and mental energies, through daily prayer, meditations, and affirmations. This taps into the little understood world of the power of thought.

Many people do not realize how powerful thought is and how to effectively use thought power for attracting positive experiences and people into their lives. How many times have you wanted something so bad that 'you could taste it?', because you took the thought to higher places, such as

The ScreamBed Chronicles

seeing yourself doing, or of having what you desired; you manifested what you desired. No, it was not a coincidence. It was as real as the creation of the universe itself, which is nothing more than a thought (in the mind of God) made real.

We use these principles everyday, doing mundane tasks such as getting up to go to work. When you hear the alarm go off, your subconscious mind see how your whole morning will manifest, the thoughts pass through so quickly, that your conscious mind does not give it a second notice. Your subconscious is the great indiscriminant recorder. It records things you are unaware of as well as the things you are aware of.

That is where the daily prayer, meditations, and affirmations come into play. They slowly de-program your subconscious and replace the old content with new content. The old content is usually everything that you have learned, everything good and bad, whether they may be thoughts of wealth, poverty, sickness, health, and self-esteem.

The old subconscious thoughts can make or break you. If you were to do an experiment with a set of twins, separate them, raise them differently, where one is constantly given positive reinforcements, while the other would be raised with

Brotha 2 Brotha

negative reinforcements and other negative thoughts. The twin raised with the positive environment would most likely be successful in business, careers, relationships, and health, while the other one will probably not be as successful in the same areas.

Thoughts are serious. The simplistic bottom-line-difference between a wealthy person and a poor person is the thoughts each person entertains. Poor people tend to overwhelmingly think and "know" that they are poor; they keep the thought cycle going on and on, making it more real for them. People in unfulfilling relationships stay in the same type of relationships because they 'know' that's 'what they deserve'.

Remember that when you do something for selfish reasons, something always seem to happen that is not too positive. So, leave the selfishness behind, bury it, and do things out of a sincere desire to change for the better. Brothas, the processes that are outlined here are quite simple to do and they are hard to do. If you are good at ignoring your own demons, friends, and even family that do not want to see you go into more positive directions, then it will be easy.

It is surprising how many of the people that you have called your close friends, react when you try to make a positive

The ScreamBed Chronicles

change. Many people tend to use other people as gauges to judge themselves. I sincerely believe that most brothas, who are not showing all of their good or God-self, really want to express their God selves, but sometimes the peer thing is so great that their egos is the deciding factor and their women usually gets the short end of the deal.

After all the self-evaluation and changes, you are ready for your girlfriend, wife, or future sista love. The good part about all of this is you are ready for experiencing the universe as a whole being. There is no more blaming others for your own behaviors, no more self hatred, no more low self esteem and no more sista dissing, whether physical, mental, or spiritual. Your ego will be much smaller and therefore more manageable, and you are ready to start a new life with your sista love.

Some sample spiritual words for learning about you:
I give thanks to God for the awareness of my whole self, for knowing the bad and the good parts of myself.
Another one:
I give thanks to God for my awakening to the realities of my innermost spirit, thoughts, and personality.

26

Brotha 2 Brotha

Here is one for change:
I give thanks to God for the positive changes that are flowing through my spirit, mind and body and for me being a better person overall. Here's another one: *I thank God for the great positive changes within me that has resulted in my being a much better person spiritually, mentally, emotionally and physically.*

Here are the spiritual maintenance words:
I give thanks to God for all the right thoughts going through me and for the continual elimination of wrong thoughts.

Another:
I give thanks to God for all the positive thoughts, energies, and people that continue to bless me and for the elimination of all negative thoughts, energies, and people from all levels of my consciousness and being.

Remember not to use my exact words, personalize them according to your feelings and energy. You should use your own prayer/ affirmation words.

Healing

healing is not an art
healing is not for a privileged few
healing can be done by u
healing is your right
to heal u must acknowledge that you are
a spiritual being, enclosed in flesh
acknowledge that the condition to heal is
not an enemy or evil condition
acknowledge that most dis-ease/ illness are
caused by the mind (i.e. wrong or harmful
thoughts about yourself or others;
unwillingness to forgive yourself or others)
acknowledge that with the power of the
Great Spirit flowing through u and love this
will be the only true way to get back to
homeostasis (balance within the body)
**cancer= animosity, holding on to
negative emotions, unforgiving
stomach problems= uncertainty about
your status n this world, anxiety immune
impairment= lack of self love or love
from others, desiring attention
female problems= self hatred, allowing
men to control excessively**

Strong Sista

sistas be strong
you are there- always
bringing forth another flesh enclosed soul
sistas be strong
u used to turn your vaginas to the sun
to get fertilized and create
now u endure the penis coming
from wherever and whomever
to create n this part of the great year
sistas be strong- u deal with some brothas
with shoulder chips and no money
u still carry your God within remembering
i sing praises to this black Goddess female
womb-man you are the energy for these
times
sistas be strong
sistas be strong
time won't be too long
for your past potential to flower
wake up the Great Spirit seed within
to participate n the Mother Earth's great
orgasm
align- align
i align- i align

A long dae in the next

she looked at me as if she liked me
but i couldn't because of...
well, the world is full of
cheaters
and i'm not the person to do it
u see, she misunderstood me
and she works nearby to my half
kind
n essence she would
at the drop of my coin
and i hesitate to answer because
well, because i remembered
something very important
pertaining to these things
that is...

Love back home

I see u
U wanted to
But I wasn't there
I see u
U wanted to
But I wasn't there
Can't get in u
Gotta love back home
She's better than u
Get away from me
Trying to entice me
With your hot violin
to get my guitar all strung up
My flowers are blooming back home
Leave me alone
I couldn't live with myself
If u had me
No-she wouldn't know
U'd just be a ho
Trying to please me
U can't please a man n love
With yo sticky vagina floor
 And big ass shore

Poem dedicated to all of the faithful
brothas.

Sex Ed: One day @ Pussy Tree

I spent my early years in Augusta, Georgia. An old city, joining a section of Georgia and South Carolina together; a city blessed with a bunch of hospitals, the 'Big Golf Game' and the Savannah River. In this big small city, my imagination was my only true friend. I remember the fun times going to my aunt's house during the summer. I was maybe, seven or eight years old, when I first noticed the tree.

Only my imagination could see what I saw on that tree. At that age, I could not have possibly seen a real one or even know what a real one looked like. Nevertheless, nevertheless, I saw it and I showed it to my younger sister and cousin. There it was

The ScreamBed Chronicles

shaped by nature and having almost perfect form. This tree growing beside my aunt's house, right next to her crooked driveway had what looked like a big pussy on it.

I do not exactly remember when I became pussy conscious. But that tree sported a big pussy and the other thing about it, the pussy was closed as if suggesting that it was a virgin pussy. Of course, I am interjecting my present views about it looking like a closed virgin pussy. I did not know what a virgin was and surely would not have known if a virgin pussy looked any different from any other kind of pussy.

Playing near the pussy tree brought snickers to my sister, cousin, and me. For a long time, we *knew* this was our major secret.

The illusion of this secrecy was shattered on one hot, nasty summer day. One of my older cousins and my daddy's stepfather's son had a secret to share with me. I was thirteen years old, eighty percent nerd and twenty percent cool. Walking across the street, I wondered what these sneaky-eyed dudes had up their sleeves. My imagination kicked in with fast car speed: maybe I am being initiated into a club. Naw, I thought, I'm just being led to the pussy tree.

The grins on their faces got bigger as we got closer to the tree. My uncle usually talked loudly, so when

Sex Ed: One day @ Pussy Tree

he adopted a hush, hush 'I'm full of secrets talk' vibe, I knew that this was not an ordinary gathering. I felt that I was being initiated into a world from which I would never escape. In his best impersonation of a sneaky character, he pointed to the pussy shape on the tree and asked me if I knew what it was.

My cousin, with an equally sneaky freaky look on his face, started snickering. My uncle was not too much older than I was, but because my family put a lot of respect and dignity into the word uncle and in the person, an uncle had almost as much respect as a father. In my young silly mind, my respect for my uncle was put in another category. Any mystery that he had as an uncle was destroyed, and at the same time, I felt a little fear. I started to feel that I was being initiated into the 'you're getting older' club. I had a bad taste in my mouth from my fears. I knew what I thought the shape on the tree *looked* like, but did I know what it was.

Was I being set up to be laughed at? Were my uncle and cousin just asking an obviously, sexually, inexperienced boy about an intimate female body part that they surely must've seen many times, to hear my response and fall out laughing?

The ScreamBed Chronicles

Well, I summoned the courage to tell them that it was a pussy. I heard a slight giggle from the right. I then felt lightheaded and a little hungry. My uncle then asked me if I had ever screwed one. Now this question really took me by surprise. Screwed one? Do they realize that I am only thirteen? Thirteen-year-olds do not screw pussies to my knowledge. We only liked to hump on girls' booties and if we got lucky, we could 'get the front side'.

I felt an overpowering urge to tell them that I had screwed a pussy before, feeling a little like an initiate of their club. I was in a nervous, silly teen mood. I allowed the word yes to slide out of my innocent mouth. My cousin jumped into overdrive with his questions about my pussy getting experience. Why would he ask that? I start drawing on serious imagination, some of my lies came to me from the sneaky readings of my mother's sex education book.

After the first word or two out of my mouth, my uncle knew I was a virgin. So, we walked into my aunt's den and I, the student was given a whirlwind sex education. It was straightforward and strangely enough, it seems as if my mother, grandmother, and aunt knew about this whole scene unfolding. My mind started its thing of non-stop questions. Did my mom

Sex Ed: One day @ Pussy Tree

and the others ask my uncle and cousin to drag me to the pussy tree just to initiate this informal 'University of Sexual Education'? Of course, my young silly ass could not be without nervous, embarrassed laughter with each description of the sexual events.

The turning point came when my uncle told me about condoms. He told me that I should put these on my dick to keep from making a baby. He told me about an internal stream that would shoot out of my dick when the sex is feeling the best. I knew about the mechanics of that from reading my mom's black sex book. But I had never experienced the stream when humping on girls around that time. I knew that the humping felt good, but why didn't my stream shoot out? I started to feel that maybe the stream would only come out if I put my dick in a pussy. Somehow, I was confused about the sex mechanics, not connecting what I had been doing in humping is essentially the same as screwing, except my dick would be in her instead of in my underwear or on her booty.

The lessons lasted for a while. My mother walked in with an 'I know what you're talking about' look on her face. She looked at my uncle and cousin and verified my

The ScreamBed Chronicles

suspicions with the question of "are y'all teaching that boy about the birds and bees?" By now, I am through, my mother knows! This cannot be happening. My uncle answered. "He'll be cool."

It was almost two years before I actually got me some, and yes, my inside stream flowed out and yes, I did have a condom on. Strangely, for the first few times that I screwed, those lessons in my thirteenth year would whisper in my ear when it was time to perform, I would then grin in the dark while mounted on top of some man's daughter. Many years later, I visited pussy tree a few times, with my first wife and then my second wife. I felt that the showing of this tree was like showing them a sacred object or something serious like that. Both times, they listened to my story, while being in awe about the way nature carved this pussy into the tree. Even though things did change, I'll never forget my nasty, sun summer, day schooling that broke the secret of pussy tree, and started me on the road to the serious study of how and at what cost I could get mo' pussy. Because I liked to feel the inside stream shooting out.

Y r u freaking?

Girl what ya doing
Why r u shaking
Yo thang n his face
Your heart is a breaking
U don't need to show it
Your mystical body
If he wants to love u
He'll get to know your heart

Baby- you're so special
U gotta pull it out-your inside
U can be strong-when you are free
U gotta pull it out-your inside

Girl why u freaking
Whimsical are u
Because he wanna do it
Don't let his boy screw it
Stay with your spirit
U only want his love
He won't do right
Kick his ass to the curb

Baby- you're so special
U gotta pull it out-your inside
U can b strong-when you are free
U gotta pull it out-your inside

Dog Brotha: One day I grew a playa

I used to be a playa. Women hear these words all the time from men. What is a playa? Would a true playa tell a woman about his past, or would he let it lie dead as a pile of dead leaves? The word playa is played out. I am sick of it. It holds no value anymore if it ever did. Furthermore, most sistas being infinitely intelligent as they are can see through the bullshit.

It is time to break down the illusion of the playa's world, to expose its bullshit. First, I need to get a few things straight. st I used to be a Pla..., I was

The ScreamBed Chronicles

the kind of brotha that just happened to enjoy being with more than one sista at a time. I played mental games, sometimes backstabbed, and told many lies to get what I wanted out of sistas.

My playa days started a little rough. I remember when I was about 14; I had a crush on one of my neighborhood friend's sisters. At the time, she was about 15, much hipper than I was and pretty as hell. She would not give me attention if I needed it to stay alive, so I decided to give her something that I knew she loved candy bars. I bought my 'girlfriend' a candy bar almost everyday for about a week. Did she let me hug her, kiss her, hold her hand, or acknowledge me? Hell no! But she did eat the candy bars as quick as I gave them to her.

I did not get any farther with her, and a few weeks later, I found out that she was drooling over this other guy. What made this bad was that I would go visit her brother to see her, and I would have to listen to her talk to her other sisters about this pretty boy. Sometimes, my love-tired (or infatuated) heart felt that she deliberately tried to hurt my feelings, but I shed no tears. I decided a little later that I would not allow any other girl to run my feelings into the ground anymore. I would not allow any future girl to get close

Dog Brotha: One day I grew a playa

to my heart and I would always present the tough as stone exterior while shielding my delicate heart. Over the next couple of years, I perfected this mentality, until it consumed me. There was no separation of me from it and I became a 'star'.

While I was no serious pretty boy, I got my share of play enough to give my head some slight inflation. I played the role hard, meeting girls and dissing them for not giving me any play; many of them were nice, some pretty and smart, and some I really wanted to be with in a relationship.

My new role would not allow me to. The mind games were Freudian to the max, especially for a late teen to early twenty-something. While many of us know that it's easy to manipulate a teenaged girl that don't know too much, and they would be right in many ways, but there were a few older women that fell for my games too. In my early twenties, I relied on younger women and some late teen girls to keep this playa thing going.

Still there were some girls that I would have seriously settled down with had I not joined the 'Playas club'. My college friends and I would rib each other for appearing soft or weak, a state of mind we called 'sad'. Sometimes I heard my friends telling their

The ScreamBed Chronicles

girls: I love you, begging their girls for sex or just for them to come visit them. I'd laugh at the sheer hipocrasy of my friends' private and public personas. The peer pressure was so intense to maintain the playa's credentials and with each new girl in my life; it was getting more difficult to hide my true feelings. In a way, I think that I may have secretly desired to have my heart broken. In fact, I even wrote a few sad songs and poetry during a certain period to cast myself in the shoes of the broken hearted.

The closest I ever came to getting my heart broken, was with a girlfriend that I had mostly good relationship with. She and I were very much alike. But I eventually wanted to manipulate her as I had the others. She was not biting. After six or seven months, we had gotten more intense and I know in my heart that she was crazy about me, but that old playa inside refused to let me grow up. Instead of me growing up, I wanted to keep 'growing down'. After much fighting in the last couple of months of our relationship, she told me to get the hell on. A girl telling me to split! This was unheard of, but it happened. Suddenly, I 'forgot' my playa's membership and tried to act right. Still she wanted no part of me.

As much as I would not admit it at the

Dog Brotha: One day I grew a playa

time, she made me look at my flawed playa theory and was the initial reason that I wanted my playa's membership revoked--for life. I ended up getting married about two and a half years later at the age of 23, and because the last girlfriend pulled a few nerves, I sought safety and devotion from my new wife. I was sort of a control freak and wanted more control.

What is it that makes some guys into control and ego freaks, while other guys release their hearts readily into the laps of some heart-eating women? In most self-proclaimed playas' minds is a fearful man. What does a man fear most about a woman? Commitment, right? Hell, we all know that! Hardly anything scares a man more than commitment. Why? At the root of commitment lies, the potential for a broken heart and many men have had their hearts broken, so by joining the playa's club, they can play the nonchalant role, while hiding behind the illusion of having many women in their lives and not giving a shit about it.

True, the average playa does maintain some sort of a relationship with many women. But how many women do these brothas want to be with, to have sex with, to take out to eat, to introduce to their mommas? Only one. In the playa's

The ScreamBed Chronicles

heart screams the 'one-woman' desire. But he is subconsciously afraid of her mind.

Man has always acknowledged woman's strength, wisdom, and beauty. The sista's mind has been the least publicly acknowledged and most feared. Maybe this is the reason that the most womanizing guys tend to separate women's body 'parts', thusly, objectifying them and refusing to see her as a wholistic being. This makes it easier for these weak-minded guys to deal with their Femalephobia (my term).

The longer a brotha remains non-committed, on the conscious level, the more he will emotionally depend on the sista that he eventually decides to commit to or marry. Most brothas will not admit their emotional dependency on their women. But it is real. Many times, when the brotha's emotions rise to the surface to be exposed, that's when they do something foolish, such as starting a silly argument, sleeping around or being physically abusive. The

Dog Brotha: One day I grew a playa

man's jealousy, anger, and inherent fear must express itself somewhere. After all, when some men see the multi-tasking sista putting up with bullshit at work *and home,* and she is still looking unfazed by it all, she becomes an easy target of his.

> Dog Brotha go into yourself
> and find your chicken heart
> Dog Brotha change the weak to the strong be free to your sista and she'll return freedom
> Dog Brotha throw spiritual love to your sista and she'll bring you into her vagina, her spiritual vagina...

I finally came to my senses in the playa game and what I realized is it boiled down to this: it is about the vagina. Case in point: If I'm with someone (she has a vagina and she allows me to make love to her), I'm sure that I'll see many other sistas that may look as good or better than her (along with their vaginas-but will they allow me to make love to them?) This becomes a new challenge. I soon realized that another vagina would not feel too different from the one that my girl has, although the potentially new 'notch on the

The ScreamBed Chronicles

belt' may have different moves when loving me. Of course, 'attached' to that other vagina is a totally different, breathing, and thinking woman. So, the question to the playa in me was why should I chase another sista just to accomplish my internal goal of putting my penis into her vagina? Wow a new vagina!

I am not trivializing women when I break down my "Vagina Theory of Similarity", of course every sista will be different because the man's mind will create the illusion based on external stimuli. In his mind, this new fine sista he's chased and finally grabbed 'felt good' and she certainly 'felt better than his girl did'.

Bottom line was, why risk something that is good and familiar to you for the conquest of something that will mostly feel similar to what you already have. As simple as the concept was, I still found myself wanting to chase women or be chased by women. This time I was not as interested in getting into 'some trouble', but a part of me (my ego) enjoyed sistas' attention and flirtatious words. Many men and women need attention from each other and if a sista is giving her man attention occasionally and vise versa; the attention seeking from others may not be a major issue.

Dog Brotha: One day I grew a playa

The bottom line is many men are very insecure within, being even more insecure than many women are. We have so many roles to play and because of the illusion that we keep going, we cannot afford to expose what we are all about. So that goes back to the beginning premise about playas being insecure. The more extreme the playa, the more insecure and dependent on a woman he is.

Rather than face his fears, insecurities and subtle hatred of women, the playa chooses to hide behind an illusion. His illusion may carry him a little way with sistas, but eventually he will commit relationship suicide, because no woman will want him after a while. The playa carries a certain energy or vibration about him and most sistas, because of their intuition, will pick up on the no-good energy and spit him out like a watermelon seed.

He will lay stunned on the sidewalk of her strong personality like a stomped roach and fail to get into her home (vagina). If he is smart, he will evaluate his life and make some major changes to his modus operandi. Life is too long to carry a playa vibe and be lonely.

Eye'll come with u

I'll come with u
I'll leave my heart behind
I'll twist it in u
Leave a love denied
Like a jazz flowing motion
And a rock dripping sulphur
We tangle like baby spiders
I get deep n your ocean
I'll come with u
If u'll leave your heart behind
I'll show u my twister
If u don't tell the outside bout the inside
I know that u'll go
Where I go
U follow the energy
I follow the magic show
Don't scream too loud
When I rope u in my freaky land
Don't bring your heart so close
Cause my twister's insane-it'll bring u pain
I'll come with u
Leave my heart behind
U show my twister a new thing
My heart's on the verge of pain
I came with u
U took my heart away
And beat me about a falling star day
With our game
Buried deep in the back
Of our pain
I know that u'll go
Where I go

The ScreamBed Chronicles

U follow the energy
I follow the magic show
The bright sunshine
Dried my 10 day tears
Wanting to die
When u stole my heart-left me fears
U used my 100 million dollars
to buy u another soul twister
on the riverbank-scream and holler
a frosty heart stomping sista
no more twister show
and 100 million dollar ho
no more twister no
for the heart stealing sista ho

Dedicated to the brothas who think they are
the playas but are the played.

Contemplation of marital suicide

years ago, i saw him at the lecture and
soul gathering
i didn't know his name
his wife was there... but i didn't see her
our definite roads crossed again
this time wife and i
became i and i
feelings from ago-long time
he was an associate going into friendom
only i wouldn't and couldn't let it evolve
because i felt a plan
because his wife felt a plan
his ego and trust shattered by the
pierce of a deception bullet
she escaped his velocity
to find herself in times of joy
of love
the money is not what it used to be
but the baby's just fine
is this real or is this the illusion grand?

Writing notes from the edge of bed

she drove me
i didn't eat for days
she asked me questions of love
only those things that r asked after the
thing
i told her no
she cried, i lied
she held me n her sunshine
everything went lavender
i started to throb past the point
she arched like a cat
screaming n unison with my screams
i told her i was involved
involved?
but why? u told me yes
she was red and turned out

Love n the air

I got a love n the air
It's coming down on me
Her mental beauty, I can't compare
Her sexy dealing, washing over me
We tell each other: don't call me
Still we come back for more
I adore her respect of what I'm in
A difficult situation

You are my mystery girl
My feelings' are not so easy
Sliding deeper n my world
Between principles & teasing

Got some love in my heart
If your patience is strong
Can feel infinity with us
With a friendship love song
Each day, our hearts grow fonder
And our minds keep the distance
Your light is beautiful-surrounding u
Let's shine our lights together

You are my mystery girl
My feelings' are not so easy
Sliding deeper n my world
Between principles & teasing

Stop flunking in girls 101

There are many single women out there. They are beautiful, bright, and economically successful women. Despite what the media is always harping on, there are many single, responsible, handsome, bright, ambitious brothas out there as well.

But, sometimes with the way both parties act, you would think that all the eligible sistas were moved to the distant planet of Standoffish and the brothas were schooled by the Hungry Dog Club. The same old, tired scenarios seem to play out between the sexes since the hot molten liquid of planet earth, cooled down enough to have God plop man and woman on its surface.

The ScreamBed Chronicles

On this planet, we have mostly been influenced to look at the way a person look on the outside, rather than feeling the spirit of that person. For instance, you have the beautiful sista with either, no special man in her life or with a special man in her life, but he does not 'look like her type'. There are various reasons for men-less women, 'mix-match' couples and women-less men. The main reasons that are being touched on in this writing also have a common cause.

Stop Flunking in Girls, man. Stop showing her the side of you that is not real. Women are in tune to the bullshit. If they do not seem to be, it is only because they choose to ignore the little voice within. Most women only want a down to earth man that looks decent for them at the least and who will treat them with kindness, compassion, and respect. Women that only seem to gravitate towards the 'sugar daddies' or super handsome model types, are in the minority and even those women when asked to go deep within their soul, would want a kind, respectful brotha.

Stop flunking in girls 101

One of my college buddies and I are hanging out at one of Atlanta's hottest clubs on a Saturday night. The music is thumping, as always, and the sistas are out in full force and I get that half-scared half-excited feeling in my stomach, as I walk through the dimly lit club.

My friend is starting to hang on to just about every sista he passes by. I am calm and cool, on the outside (as always) although I admit that the sistas' big asses and thighs bursting through their skirts are starting to arouse the dog. I speak to a few sistas while gently rocking my head to the music.

I may be one of the strangest guys as far as clubbing goes, because I rarely dance when I go out. In fact, I have only danced one good time in my entire clubbing life (which was not too extensive). I only went to clubs to meet women, get telephone numbers, and get laid. My friend has found his first victim for the night. A tall, caramel colored honey with a dining room table ass and 'painted' on mini skirt (yes! it's fitting her that well). My friend is starting his thing of "you so gorgeous and fine, I would love to get to know you", and "let's dance".

The ScreamBed Chronicles

She looks at him as if she just received a telemarketing call during dinnertime. I step further into the shadows to see the 'I only want to get her in bed show'. Then my friend starts telling her about the money that he's making and what he is doing for a living. Keep in mind, I do not remember her even giving him more than her name, and that's it. After about 30 minutes of advertising his 'virtues', he asked for her number. There is a pause, and then the nerve shaking answer is delivered: "No, you're not my type." My friend is still trying to get her number by hyping himself higher. She insists, no.

Now, this sista is hot and my friend did not get too far with her, so I keep my eye on her for a few moments. The music is thumping harder and is providing the perfect backdrop for my 'verbal painting'. Walking up to this fine honey, I cannot help but notice her architecture: tall (about five eight or so), big, beautiful eyes, luscious lips, and a smile that will melt a skyscraper. She sees me. I smile. She smiles. My heart races and my mind braces. (*Words... must say some words*). I introduce myself. She small talks about my friend and laughs. She asks, "Are you from Atlanta?" Atlanta. "No", I say.

Stop flunking in girls 101

"I'm a just a strange country boy." She's from Michigan and has been in Atlanta for about two years. After telling her that I'm from Augusta and seeing her disbelieving face, I tell her that I'm not from Augusta, I'm from Saturn and I've only lived on earth for about 160 years. She laughs hard.

We talk on and on into the funky music night. Subjects such as art, music, philosophy, writing, and even God were touched on. After about an hour of talking and no dancing, it was time to leave, so I told her goodbye, "Hope to run into you again", I said. As I spat out the last word, she offered me her number and asked for mine. She had to keep in touch with me, because she wanted to "continue our conversations", she said. My friend walked up as me, and the honey was exchanging numbers. He glared at her and had the audacity to utter the words: "I can't believe you want to be bothered with him. He can't spend the money on you like I can". Of course, he said it in a playful tone to play off his bruised ego, but she just looked at him and looked at me, and then laughed.

The ScreamBed Chronicles

Over the next several weeks, we got to know each other 'very well'. Even though our friendship did not evolve into a more serious relationship, this true story is repeated everyday where ego-drenched men are selling their external selves to women, and the real, down to earth men are racking up the women and maintaining solid relationships.

As strange as my look and views have been, I have not had a hard time hooking up with women. When a sista would meet me, she would meet *me*. She would see a man that has an artistic, eclectic look, have a different outlook on life and embrace the bizarre. She would meet a geek that loves talking about quantum physics, architecture, and computers as much as most people love talking about the current events. I would not have to pose a certain way in public, you know the, oh so cool brotha look. If, while I am walking, I trip a little, I would laugh about it without feeling un-cool or goofy. This is a part of my personality. That is all I can be.

While the above story does not represent most men-women meeting situations, the one thing that is constant is just be yourself. The way a man looks does matter in terms of success or failure in meeting women. The way that a man relates, by talking to women also, determines his

Stop flunking in girls 101

success, but his sex appeal is probably bigger than his looks. Sex appeal does not necessarily mean that the man is (in the words of many sistas) a 'cutey'. He may capture sistas with his eye contact or poetic words. He may move as smooth as an eagle; whatever the case is, many women will find it hard to say no to this kind of brotha.

Brothas, if you do not have natural sex appeal, whatever you do to suggest otherwise will fail, you will look as if you are trying too hard. But on the flip side, if you do have loads of sex appeal and try to *deny* it, this can make you even *more* attractive to sistas. Go figure. Does having a great sex appeal equal to having a lot of sex? No, yes or maybe. It depends on if the guy have the 'intent disguise ability.' This is the ability to meet a fine sista, damn well knowing that you want her, but you act as if you do not.

In the earlier club scene, the fine sista with the dining table a.., you know who I am talking about. I was initially attracted to this woman based on her exterior dimensions, I did not know if her breath stank, if she had rotten teeth, funky toes or if she picks her nose. I knew only about what I saw and that was that ferocious back-end. A back-end that I had already

The ScreamBed Chronicles

found room in my nasty mind to eventually get a piece of. I'm sure that she knew my intentions (as most women do), but for me to be blatant about it as my friend was, smacks short of asking her to go to a hotel room and having some hot sex.

Of course, the sexuality of the meeting was neutralized by good conversation, which has always been the main ingredient of my 'intent disguise ability'. Men and women know instinctively that the purpose of meeting each other is to get into somebody's bed and play the hump game. And why do we like playing the hump game? To make babies and keep the human race going. It is in man's genetics to go after that 'thang' and it is in woman's genetics to make us work for it.

Society of course makes sistas feel guilty about their own sexual needs and urges, so you will have some sistas that will make some men jump off bridges and climb the Empire State Building to get some. That is guilt on steroids. But brothas, if you want to get anywhere with the sistas, it will help if you disguise your intent somewhat. Now I do not want the sistas angry with me for what seems to be me advising brothas to deceive them to get into their pants (I am not doing this). I realize that sex is a major part of the game, and I know that sistas play to brothas

Stop flunking in girls 101

wants and needs (as well as theirs) by the way they look and dress (make-up, revealing and form-fitting clothing). I only want to expose the deeper bottom line. Maybe, if I express it differently if would sound better: brothas do as the sistas do, downplay your true sexual feelings and urges and express them at a more appropriate time.

Brothas are you ready to go clubbing so that you can get some 'good stuff' or are you ready to open your minds and expand your dimensions, so that you can have quality rather than quantity. There is someone for everybody. If you go for everybody, you usually end up with no one. Remember that women are infinitely smarter than YOU are. When they want you, THEY will CHOOSE you.

Remember your sex education class back in the day, regarding the actions of sperm and egg cells. When a man ejaculates inside a woman during sex, there are millions of fast swimming, aggressive sperm cells in a drop of semen. They are all racing to get one egg most of the time. The egg chooses which sperm cell is going to fertilize it. The fastest arriving sperm cell is not guaranteed to fertilize the cell. Women

The ScreamBed Chronicles

instinctively KNOW on a genetic level, which man is genetically better to fertilize her egg(s).

Sex is an overrated subject in American society. It is overrated because only the basic design or basic structure of sex (i.e. the physical act and physical urges for booties, thighs, and breasts) is emphasized. Most popular culture emphasizes the physical aspects of sex. In many women's minds, the possibility of meeting a man bring with it, the possibility of romance, love and eventually children. So, sex is used as the bait, to attract and reel in a man.

According to most women, many men do not like to do much foreplay (or at least the amount that women need for basic arousal). Many sex surveys also show that many men do not care whether their significant other feel satisfied or have an orgasm. What is wrong brothas? If you want to stop flunking in girls, you need to do a 180-degree turnaround. There is entirely too much blame coming from the brothas regarding why their women are not 'getting theirs'. There are too many sex-lazy men that want to roll over like a big dripping bear after his squirt gun goes off.

Stop flunking in girls 101

There are too many brothas that do not know how to tenderly massage, touch, and caress their women. Many sistas want to be caressed. Many men also do not ALLOW their feminine selves to be expressed with their women and that is part of the reason why many, if not most women, are unsatisfied in their relationships. Many women need their man to be a little gentle, occasionally. Brotha, it is time to change the course of your ship. You may get her into bed and 'bang a few screws', but if you're not feeling her, then you won't have her too long.

Brothas, get into your woman like how you feel your ride. The same compassion and the love that you feel for your ride or your wheels, you need to triple that feeling toward your woman. Shower her with sweet words every day. Pepper her with sentences that speak of the care and love that you have for her. If you do not love her yet, then tell her how much you appreciate her essence and mind. Brotha, feel good about the fact that no matter what your age is, you chose this point in time to stop flunking in girls; you chose to change your way of thinking, your way of meeting sistas, your way of having sex. You did not change because it was the latest fad or trend; you

The ScreamBed Chronicles

changed because you want to be a joy to your woman or potential woman. You wanted to retire an old, crusty, dusty model of what the world said men should be like, and go in the direction of being more of an ideal man.

Remember in order to stop looking as a fool, you must keep in mind these very important points: Women are stronger and smarter than you are (how do I know and why do I keep expounding on this point?) For instance, if an emergency came up with a close to term pregnancy, where the woman could not get to a hospital when it is time to deliver; she could have a baby without ANY medical intervention. That is strength and intelligence. How many men do you know that would be able to withstand three months of morning sickness that some sistas experience in pregnancy, much less carry a baby for nine months. There are many instances of men fainting at the mere mention of their woman going into labor.

Remember that women like sex just as much if not more (when it is good) than men do. When brothas do not express their whole self in the sex moment, the true power of the connection between the vagina and penis is not fully realized. There are some men that are wholistic

Stop flunking in girls 101

in their approach to sex and those are the brothas that are snatching and keeping women like there's no tomorrow. The main point to remember is the intuitive ability of sistas. If more sistas realized that they are naturally more intuitive, they would not be held captive by the illusion that they are the weaker sex, or that they do not deserve good things. They would know how to anticipate our every move when needed.

Much of this was written back in 1989, when I was 23 years old. Now I am much older and the 'man meets woman' scene is a little different, and in some ways, it is still the same. There is desperation on both sides. Many women are desperate for love, true sexual connection, understanding, and respect. Many men seem desperate for many different pieces of cake and more vagina experiences. Yes, many men seem to be still flunking in girls.

The pregnant woman in the tub

i watched through the cracked door
a pregnant woman bathing
a dripping faucet and splashing tub singing
to me back and forth
this pregnant woman's breasts were full of
colostrum
and they were glistening under the water
the air smelled of burning candles and soap
my desires made me smell her vagina
with each graceful move to clean herself
i would grab my penis
and hold it tight to keep it from bursting
out of my drawers
it was a nasty scene mixed with pure
glamour girl

Kinda love thang

Show me yo underwear
Gotta act like I care
Show me yo underwear
Gotta act like I care
Everything's in speed motion
Making my move
to take a drink of yo ocean
I'll make your body groove
U spend yo time with yo makeup
Wriggling in yo tight skirt
Do U have a pierced tongue
If U do, show me what U do
Baby you kinda young
Not too young for me to do
What U expect, U give it up
Like a money ho
Trading self esteem
for fake love in your door
U spend yo time with yo makeup
Wriggling in yo tight skirt
Now U started drinking juice
Then later U started smoking sticks
to impress yo artificial man
swollen belly & getting sick
his nervous sweat in yo eye
he says U too young
to have one now
but wasn't too young to lay down
U spend yo time with yo makeup
Wriggling in yo tight skirt
Some men are like flies on shit
When they see a tight skirt

The ScreamBed Chronicles

Their thinking is below
You're thinking mostly above
U think it's love
Because he gives U a feeling
But he may give others that feeling
He just likes the feeling
U spend yo time with yo makeup
Wriggling in yo tight skirt

Song dedicated to all the young girls and
women looking for love in all the wrong
places.

Your rivers of explosion tunes: Respect of the closed legs

your beauty fills me with a lust
but i know your rules
i can feel your mind
i beg for your physicality
but i know your rules
your body shape slithers into my ego dream
still begging for some-- time
and i still know your rules
after our minds meet
our bodies greet
on our night, i realize your head
on our night, i experience your wholeness
u caress me
u bless me
u become me
i become u
merging rivers n the cosmic forest
explosion
your music is the best- the only
there's no other music- for me
all the other songs sound the same
your love keeps me out of the rain

Y eye wasn't a girl

i knew that i wouldn't go through it... again
i got an understanding about the female
seems to me she kinda ran things on all the
planes
until the pop people came into power
power of the pussy
too much power
no steam to drive forth the power
make up
big asses and tiny toes
it was good when i was... she
i understood love
i felt pretty n the mirror
but that was eons ago (there were no
mirrors)
maybe 30,000 years before this
brothas remember your vagina days
helps u stay in good with your love
and your love stay good
r-e-s-p-e-c-t women
star guides to the soul
your mother today
maybe your wife tomorrow
i knew i wasn't going through with it again
besides i like mine outside my body
forget all of this
i was an ego dog
i had to learn about heartbreak and love
part of my lesson was to do a few rounds
to get the grade and the weight...

Affairs, platonic relationships, and other things

When you hear the word affair, what do you see? Do you imagine a scene where a man and woman are 'messing around' at the office? Maybe you see a homemaker screwing the plumber or her neighbor. While these images do represent different aspects of affairs, however, affairs are usually much deeper than the above scenarios. They can range from two people having a need to be around each other all the time, (sex may not even be in the picture) to long, deep relationships that do include sex.

When I reflect on my life in the past, I thought that I had 'friendships' with

The ScreamBed Chronicles

women. But I later found out that my 'friend' adored me and would have jumped in my pants had I initiated it. Affairs are tenacious creatures that can sneak up on one of the innocent parties in the 'friendship'. I have always felt more comfortable around women and generally have had more women friends. But past wives and girlfriends have had problems with me having almost exclusive female friends.

I have always had my own definition of an affair and because of that, I may have caused my past girlfriends and wives a certain amount of stress, when it came to having female friends.

What is an affair? Are they strictly emotional in nature or do they need sex or other forms of intimacy to make it technically an affair? Can an affair exist with only one of the two consciously knowing the intent of the relationship? What separates the emotional or mental affair from the platonic relationship?

I will admit that I had been naïve about women and their intentions. I have always maintained to my past wives that it takes two to 'mess around'. Is this true? Is it possible for a guy to mislead his female friend into believing that his intentions are truly platonic? Maybe he gives off a vibe to make it look like the two of them are in an

Affairs, platonic relationships, and other things

intimate relationship when around others; especially those who may have some suspicions about them, would a female co-worker always make herself known as my friend to cement an idea that we are an item, even though that's far from the truth? People have done these things many times and all this behavior is just another variation of 'I can't really have him or her the way I want him or her, so I'll play the role in public'.

This relationship form is what I would call a pseudo-affair. Usually only one person is aware of the game, the other person is being manipulated. This manipulation does not necessarily make a victim out of the other person; he or she is usually enjoying the friendship and any perceived benefits of the friendship, so victim status would not apply to them.

The ScreamBed Chronicles

Usually the person's spouse or significant other will bestow the victim crown on their 'poor' sweetie because they are jealous of the attention that is directed toward their spouse or significant other. They need to rally around something negative in the friendship to make their sweetie feel as though they have been taken advantage of and thus end the friendship.

There have been many debates about the validity of this type of friendship eventually evolving into a real affair. Only if both parties are feeling each other to the degree to initiate a real, full-blown affair, will this happen. Keep in mind that an affair is not a different kind of relationship, it has the same life cycles as any other relationship,- with one major difference of course- somebody is married or in another type of serious relationship while engaging in the activities of this new relationship. Secrecy and deception being the key ingredients.

In this society, affairs are nearly as frequent as so-called legitimate relationships. How can they not be? Men and women are apart for many hours a day, five or more days a week. Friendships develop between men and women on the job. As the comfort levels increase between male-female co-workers, the truth is slowly revealed. Then the fine, *formerly*, happy-with-her-man sista, is suddenly boo-hoo-ing

Affairs, platonic relationships, and other things

on her co-worker's shoulder about what is wrong with her man and marriage. Many times, the male friend will offer her some advice, but mostly he is listening to her. Eventually he will speak about the unhappy state of his marriage (to make his coworker feel a little better).

Eventually, enough notes are compared between the two that they slowly realize that they have many things in common and they understand each other 'better than their spouses do'. Of course, the two do not think about why they get along so well. The platonic friends do not think about the fact that they are not living with each other. The woman does not have to ask her co-worker everyday to pick up his dirty clothes off of the bedroom floor, or to raise the toilet seat when pissing. The man does not have to see his co-worker woman friend without her makeup and hair 'did'.

Their spouses know them; the relationship may not be a challenge or something exciting to them anymore. However, if the coworkers were to get together, the new relationship would probably evolve to the type of relationship that they are complaining about. The affair

The ScreamBed Chronicles

is the direct result of losing sight of the true intent of the married couple's purpose. The affair is the result of being one dimensional with a relationship.

Popular media may be partly to blame for this one-dimensionality in male-female relationships. A common scenario in many movies usually show a man and a woman meeting as friends and eventually the two develop intimate feeling, and then they fuck in a moment of 'passion.' Then they start a long-term relationship. These movies always made me wonder if a man and woman can meet, have fun, and not always evolve the relationship into a sexual thing. It would be a strictly platonic friendship.

Many couples disagree about what a platonic relationship is. I have had platonic friendships in the past (though not many) and I have never questioned the validity of the women and myself being friends. It was only when someone made a point to call out the potential of something 'deeper' with the friendship. Past girlfriends who had issues with my platonic friendships always cast me as the victim (you are so naïve; she really wants you for more than a friend). People usually cannot see a man and a woman being just friends.

Affairs, platonic relationships, and other things

How do I know that all my so-called platonic friendships were platonic coming from the woman's perspective? I do not know for sure. All I know is that most of these platonic girlfriends did not end up in my bed, naked and sweaty. Did you catch that? I said, "The majority", meaning that I did cross the line with a few of my 'platonic' friends.

Which brings up a point, were the women, my platonic friends at the time of my screwing them or did they move over to the realm of just 'friend' after screwing them. Usually when people see the word friend surrounded by quotation marks, they usually assume that the person being referred to as friend is a no-zoner; (meaning that she/he is neither a significant other or a platonic friend) but she/he is sexually involved with you. The point I am trying to get across is that we need to break out of the boxes of labeling friends and girlfriends.

Maybe, the word platonic was created to make our girlfriends and wives feel better about that annoying woman friend that always seemed to demand attention from

The ScreamBed Chronicles

us. Of course, the platonic wars were waged, pitting the true believers of men/women as friends against the 'you can't bullshit a bullshitter' group. I did not like this debate at all. It forced me to evaluate all my women friends, almost getting me on the defense about the value in having them as friends.

After much ripping and tearing of the fabric of my friendships with women, my conclusion was, I grew up with a momma and two sisters; I was pretty close to them and because of that, I felt more comfortable with women...as friends. Please do not misinterpret my words, I have men friends and associates, and I respect these friendships. I think that I will always have more women friends because I am not the typical male. In other words, I express both my masculine and feminine energies almost equally. Women are looking for a decent man to talk to and not to be talked at. They need a man that can be their friend-without them being too concerned about him trying to screw her. They need intellectual conversation many times-without sports and other macho conversations being the rule.

Maybe, if society throws out the word platonic and substitute the word friend, wives, and girlfriends, may not feel that a sista-friend is so special. The

Affairs, platonic relationships, and other things

word platonic can be a suspicious word. A platonic friend should be no different from any other friend. Do wives and girlfriends think that the word platonic would keep any woman from trying to evolve the relationship into something heavier?

Some sistas have suggested that when men say that the friendship is strictly platonic, then he may be hiding a potential affair or even an active affair behind the word. But many men who are in real platonic friendships would probably find it difficult to tell their girlfriend or wife that their woman friend is a friend, rather than platonic friend.

The word 'friend' (there goes those quotation marks again) may make many women feel that this friend may be a sex partner or love interest. And the word platonic makes men must be on the defensive about why they are using this special word for this so-called non-special woman. There lies the big paradox. Even within the confines of a regular friendship between a man and woman, are the issues of boundaries. I've had past girlfriends and wives speak about the need for me to set boundaries with my women friends.

The ScreamBed Chronicles

Fine, I would say, my boundaries are NO SEX and NO KISSING. "Oh no!" Would be the reply, "that's not enough". No long phone conversations, no late calls, not too many lunches together, and no occasional hanging out at places such as bookstores, art galleries, or concerts. Of course, real hanging out places like clubs and fancy restaurants are definitely a no-no. I did not hang out with my women friends at clubs or fancy restaurants, but every once in a while, we would go to the bookstore or art galleries.

The problem with setting boundaries is different people have different ideas about what is appropriate and what is not. Most women would not think twice about their men talking to one of his boys on the phone for an hour (if there are men that talk on the phone that long), unless it's his woman friend. Remember there should be no distinction between the friendships of men and men and women and men, if the intent of the relationship has been firmly established in the man/woman's friendship.

I do think that the issue of boundaries should be handled in a personal manner. If a man has issues with his woman about the boundaries she may or may not have with a male friend, cutting off contact with her friend may not be a good idea. Compromise is something that should be explored.

Affairs, platonic relationships, and other things

We must look at the whole picture of friends and boundaries on a deeper level. This is where I will get deep and go off on a tangent. What if one of your life's lessons is to learn patience and be more trusting of others? Better yet (deeper still), what if you chose the very life that you are in, with all its challenges, vices, temptations and sadness, to help you evolve spiritually?

The following words will probably seem contradictory to what is in the preceding paragraphs. If the words seem foreign or contradictory to your belief system, it does not suggest anything negative about you or your intelligence level. Everyone is on a different vibe, spiritual path, and spiritual understanding. The words dealing with affairs, platonic relationships and boundaries need to be absorbed by most folks.

The ScreamBed Chronicles

Remember, there are ALWAYS alternative realities and these realities may seem strange because of our past conditioning. When in doubt or when there is much confusion and frustration, just ask the universe, i.e. God, your angels, spirit guides, etc.

Sideways eight

we've been together
for a thousand years
our love is stronger
without the tears
our sun shines brightly
no cloudy fears
my love's such a beauty flower (repeat 4
times)
my thoughts are of u
though i never say
the feelings together
and i hardly say
high creator's n our hearts
to complete the bond
the music created
the children's song
my love's such a beauty flower (repeat 4
times)
WHEN I'M AROUND U
MY HEART'S ALL A POUNDING U
IMAGINE THE DREAMS
YOUR BODY'S THE SCENES, CHILLS AND SCREAMS
I LOVE U- I NEED U
our love is a sideways eight
our love is a sideways eight

Underground smiles: fuel midnight desires

I care about u...as my morning sunshine
Feeling your spirit and mine merging into one
I know that I've known u throughout time
There's no other woman for me, you're the one
Thinking of u:
You make me speak like an animal, with no language
A cloud and much rain
I'm holding u and my heart's satisfied
On a heaven level
Giving each other powers to see
Through the flowers and cards
And feel painless hearts and mental orgasms
When I touch u:
U make me climax deep n my head
Quivering like a strong tree n a windy forest
Your smiles fuck my old dog into death
Your lips are Indian rainbows, pecking my native neck
You're my baby, my heart, my desires
When I breathe, I breathe in your body, mind and soul
I desire your capture of me
Your love opening, pulling me into your deepest inside
I desire your emotions, and my emotions becoming

The ScreamBed Chronicles

E Motion
I send out a thought ray to u
I am U
U are me
We be, what we only see
We float on the waves powered by love, compassion and caring
Controlling their outcomes
COME GROW WITH ME...
To my girlfriend who agreed with me that we won't say it, but we'll play it, defining something that is slippery and boxy at the same time. That's our thing, but we're recreating things all the time that's y I want her n my life, helping me to count the cheese from our ideas and maybe n the future, become my.... This girlfriend/roommate/friend person's image in my head is influencing me to keep writing jingle jangle love type shit, that somehow feels like insurance to my heart and instant sex to my fingers...

Can't stay away from each other

When I thought of u
Coming into my mind
Then I saw u
So beautiful and divine
-Your spirit so sweet
-Your voice is so meek
And then I touched u
Knowing things wouldn't b the same
Picking cozmyk flowers
Massaging your soul with time
Minutes turn to hours
When we merge our body and mind
-I miss u so much
-When I don't feel your touch
But when I touch u
I can't help myself; u can't help yourself
Baby, we can't stay away from each other
And I don't know what to say
We can't stay away from each other
Not a single hour or day
We can't stay away from each other
Still, I don't know what to say
We can't stay away from each other
The hours turn into days
When I lay with u
Looking at our starry sky
Then I see your face
And mine, in the moonlight
-Your love is so strong
-your voice whisper a song

The ScreamBed Chronicles

And then I loved u
Stars over our heads, grass as our bed
Baby, we can't stay away from each other
And I don't know what to say
We can't stay away from each other
Not a single hour or day
We can't stay away from each other
Still, I don't know what to say
We can't stay away from each other
The hours turn into days

My organic girl

the other morning i awaken
to a power out blinking clock
i correct my time and remember the dream
it was a delicious dream
it was a girl-but not that kind of dream
she had much beauty and much mind
her heart was as light as a few molecules
her love shone as bright as the sun
she was an organic girl
her hair was original and textured
her rhythm was on the cosmic level
i knew i needed her
my organic girl
when she would look at me
my heart would drip all over my lap
as her sun-star eyes pierced my confidence
i was afraid of this organic girl
for she could make me lose my world
her love consciousness would teach me a
new respect for sistas
my organic girl would help anybody that
needed it
without money or questions
i steered this dream as best as i could
but couldn't find out about us n time
this organic girl whipped my mind
the two of us being together was whole
her mission n her earth-life being mine
her love for the rest of us being as mine
we fell in love
the trees bowed and flowers bloomed
furry creatures came from above and about

The ScreamBed Chronicles

my forever sunshine had entered the void
my soul's renewal had begun
my heaven reality was extinguished by the
push of my wife's leg against mine
introducing a private hell- lying next to me
another work day and my organic girl on
the other side
waiting for me
i was mad at my wife for divorcing me from
my organic girl
n my astral travel picture
but i know that somewhere out there in
dimension four
is my organic girl

White girls and black boys

Brothas close your eyes

and say the words: 'white woman'. Let the words bounce around in your head for a few seconds. Do you see what I used to see back in the day? Do you see a speeding top-down convertible sports car on a winding mountain road, with a beautiful woman with long, blond hair flying in the wind? She is smiling, with a touch of confidence, sensuality, and innocence. Is this one of your white woman images? Alternatively, *can* you imagine a white woman with two or three children on welfare, with no car, no status and out of shape?

The ScreamBed Chronicles

When the word 'black woman' is played in your head for a few seconds, can you see the first image without the long blond hair, white skin, but replaced with a chocolate or caramel beauty with a low cut natural or dredlocks? Many brothas, if not in a state of denial, would admit to mostly seeing the white woman in the first scenario. The image of the sista would be mostly, a heavy-set church-going woman, probably harassing the brotha to attend. The stereotypical black woman image also may involve her having much 'attitude and no gratitude' or of being snobby and career driven with no time for a brotha 'beneath her'. Of course, many brothas have many different images, some going from very positive to very negative.

The white woman's societal image is mostly of innocence, and beautiful sensuality, and in some places, being involved with a black man: taboo. Back in the day, during my 'white girl period', my friends seemed a little concerned that I was not meeting or having intimate relationships with black girls. Despite me assuring them that, it was not that I did not want to meet black girls, my situation at the time made it easier to meet

White girls and black boys

white girls. Black girls did not come my way; maybe I had a face that falsely said that I only date white girls. Was I being hooked to the drug of the 'sexually irresistible' and taboo white girl?

There were not any differences between them and sistas, except the ones that I dealt with seemed to be a little on the obsessive and possessive side (more so than the sistas I had been dealing with at the time). The only other thing that I noticed is that most of them did not seem to put up a fight about too many things, which is what I liked and needed at the time. After all, who needs an independent and headstrong woman, when you can have a woman that will 'worship your words good or bad and make you feel glad when you might be sad'? Of course, these words are not generalizations about white women; they only represent my experiences with the dozen or so white girls that I was involved with.

So, to the people who may think that I am a white girl hater, I have been there, done that. After I got over the jungle fever, I married a sista, got a divorce, and married another sista. I got my 'Declared Free of White Women for Ten Years'

The ScreamBed Chronicles

certificate a few years back, although they try to temp me every other green moon with smiles, hugs, and heavy flirting. There is nothing like having a strong sista by your side when your life is chaotic. Many of the sistas (including my two ex-wives) in my past contributed to my growth and development, they each had a part in my learning to be more responsible and above all, I learned to respect all women more.

A sista friend once told me that most white women that are intimately involved with brothas are racists. "Racists?" I asked with a slightly crooked eyebrow and impatient tone to my voice. How could they be racists when they are dealing with brothas? She screamed, "You said it right, they're just dealing with brothas". Thoughts started falling out the folds of my brain and I briefly saw where she was coming from. Is this part of the 'white man's plot' in maintaining control over black families potential for success?

In my conspiracy head, I saw a group of high-ranking, white folks meeting in an underground chamber under the auspices of certain secret societies, to discuss ways of destroying all hopes of the black family being stronger and cohesive. In my imagination, I see a woman come from the

White girls and black boys

corner of the room, dressed in a mini skirt, high heels, long hair, full lips, tanned skin, junk in her trunk and a bag of tricks. She says to one of the 'big boys', I am your number one weapon against the resurrection of the black family. One guy asks, "I thought we had crack and malt liquor on that case"? The first guy replies, "We did, but there were many people in the black community that wouldn't even touch the stuff; but this 'pretty woman' is harder to resist for the brothers. "I, the white woman can wreck a few careers and homes if I do it right".

I decided that my friend may be a little on the paranoid side. As I am sure that there are many brothas and white women that fall in love with each other, have loving families and live happily ever after.

Many years ago at a former job, I was holding a sports magazine that had a white model wearing a bikini on its cover; one of my white woman co-workers, made a comment regarding the woman and went on to suggest this cover girl was my dream or fantasy girl. My then

The ScreamBed Chronicles

smart ass said, "not really". She looked at me as if I told her that her breath stank. She could not understand why I would turn down what she probably thought most brothas would have scrambled to go after.

Then there is the legendary internet story about the white woman that had the audacity to write to a major black women's magazine talking about the love that she had for her black man and how sistas are dissing her because they are jealous. Her pen got fiery before she stopped writing; she told sistas why the brothas are jumping ship to white women, saying many stereotypical things about black women. That was stupid. Then a brotha replied with a sista- hyping and loving letter in the next issue. He effectively and tactfully dissed the white girl/ black boy combos that are not about love as much as they are about posing and using each other.

Over the past few decades, many more white women are dating, marrying, and flirting with brothas. Is this something new? Hell no, this desire has always been there, but today's world is more tolerable.

White girls and black boys

Throughout history, some white women have desired brothas from the first time they laid eyes on us and through the ages, the tolerance levels increased towards involvement that is more romantic. It is amazing how the mass media will say that black men are on the 'endangered' list due to incarceration, substance abuse, homosexuality, and outright laziness. On the other hand, I am starting to see many white women with some decent brothas. Where does that leave the sistas?

In a perfect world, race should not matter. We are all just a bunch of souls that are in different colored 'gloves' or bodies. We are living in different parts of the world, with different languages, customs, and experiences, but we have a few things in common, we hurt (whether it is physically, emotionally, mentally). We need to eat and drink water, we have sex, we need to love and receive love, and we need to sleep and dream. What if having some differences among humans, is a way that God tests our ability to love one another unconditionally?

What if each race has inherent qualities and faults that the Creator designed to allow for us to experience and transcend

The ScreamBed Chronicles

the faults. Race is nothing but an illusion anyway, it's a classification designed by curiosity, but defined by much fear. We are all a bunch of human mutts, fighting about how much 'pure blood' some of us have, funny thing is anthropologists discovered decades ago that all humanity derive from a common ancestor on the African continent. Ethnicity is determined NOT by external features, but by what's flowing on the inside of you: the many generations of sexual unions that's made an imprint on what eventually made you to be who you are. One day, many people beyond the anthropologists and other scholars, will eventually realize that race has no merit in the big picture of universal consciousness.

RedFlower: 710 secrets n the city

Who is this shawty?
Blond wavy hair...a sneaky smile
What's yo name girl?
I wanna whisper to u...something that is good.
are u from the stars or the mountains? Why do I feel this way?
Your smile make me forget my old dog ways
It makes it easy to eat your fish, look at myself.
Secrets...I don't know u that well
But I know I know u very well...we may go back awhile.
U can be addictive. My medicine...
I'm not used to feeling this way. Running away was easy.
What's inside of u? U have my attention...u didn't even try.
Scary Libra woman...keep yourself.
I'll see more of u...not own u, u not me.
I wanna grow u, grow me, in the moonflower ocean
Bathe...glow in the sun
Pick a flower until infinity...

The ScreamBed Chronicles

Hara Ffahg: I wonder if u...

I was sitting at my desk, eyes gazing at the ceiling, thinking...
Thinking about this special feeling...this feeling I get when I
Think about this woman, this woman is special, she's hot
Images of her face bring waves of joy to me....
This special woman makes me feel like no other has.
When I hold this special woman, I feel complete...full of love.
This woman is my dessert, she's my topping, she's my completion.
I send a love vibration from eternity to eternity...to this special one.
I've caught some feelings...that I'm not too familiar with
Feelings that are deep as the dark of the cosmos.
I desire this deep woman...desires that explode within me
I want this woman
feel me, touch me, love me....

The best ocean that I've swam n

Making love to u...is like the feeling of being in the ocean warm, salty water, moving in and out, between my legs the water caressing my penis, eventually expressing my juice my body jerking like an epileptic fit

38

Woman u pull out the best n me
Saving it, for your nurturing
Your ocean, so sweet and salty
I love the rolling of my tongue in your waves Lapping up ur essence, sharing in your musical explosion

Caressing your gentle curves, feeling your face, and reading your eyes

23

Such a woman with a ready smile and moist heart

Massaging your baby back, licking your curving back, while nibbling your juicy melon my penis, is connected to your electricity, it rises in temperature

U permit it to enter your swirling ocean...it's boiling waves

I'm surfing in your waves and we brace ourselves to land

A feeling rises from the bottom of your feet

A feeling rises from my ankles

We become aware of our landing

The ScreamBed Chronicles

Our feelings, so intense, we can't seem to focus
Heart beats act as big nasty drums
Punctuating our body vibrations...as we land
Feeling each other as we discover more of what we want to know

Organic girl (the hill section spoken of)

i think i found her
closing my eyes- she stood there
dangling as a whisper in october rain
she pulled my covers off
as naked as my soul was
i was still in confidence
maybe it was my sun ra playing box
that kept my confidence spilling
she was real
i started to wonder about what she would
do now
i clearly saw her mind with my heart
as her eyes danced through my naked soul
we walked barefoot through the dew grass
at the hill
we knew instinctively that the hill was ours
this early moon morn
i felt the afraidness
because she found me here
and here was a far away place from there
she could no longer hold back the woman
i could no longer hold back the man
but we held each other through the front
we began to sprout within and around one
another
our trees grew rapid smart
her electricity of particular vibration
raced through my heart
almost passing the big river
she spilled around me

The ScreamBed Chronicles

the trees were completely entwined
as the wind slowed to a whisper
she peeled her fruit away
nature pianos n the distance
give us our choice sounds
we leave the hill and the lower sun
behind   two   memories   of   our   magic
electricity

The PlayaSista underground

Many men do not want to admit it, but sistas fuck around too. They cheat, they play, and they screw other men. Those other men may look handsome or they may be average looking. Maybe these other brothas may have an ear to listen to YOUR woman. Maybe they are NOT so much into themselves as YOU may be. Sistas may not fool around as much as the brothas do, but they do. All you have to do is look back in history with the invention of the chastity belt in the early 1400's. Women screwing around had to get so bad (at least in the minds of men) that a man had to invent that hideous looking belt.

The ScreamBed Chronicles

Women of all races, classes and religions do it, whether one may find a higher propensity of messing around in certain races or classes, that question is for another book.

Most of the women that do screw around may be doing so because of a breakdown in the relationship. She is not getting something out of the relationship that is essential to her being fulfilled. There is a minority of women who stray, that are sista dogs. They could be in the most fulfilling relationship, but they still stray. In the first example of the type of straying woman, much of this straying could be eliminated, if the brotha is truly being a true man.

This is not to be confused with being super macho, but it means that men should acknowledge the masculine and feminine energies that are within them. This is not about being bi-sexual. When a man acknowledges his feminine side, which is when he is showing compassion, affection and creativity.

Many sistas would like brothas to show those traits from time to time. It does not make the brotha a soft man, but more of a total man. All humans have dual gender energies within. When the gender energy is out of balance, then the person subconsciously looks for the mate that will

The PlayaSista underground

bring balance back to them. For example, when a highly macho man is attracted to a timid woman. The timid woman is in his life to show by example, the balance he needs, to counteract his overly macho self.

Some men will show their softer side in the beginning of a relationship and as the relationship matures, they will usually revert to expressing mostly their masculine side. This change in affection towards his woman is one of the reasons why his woman may stray. If a woman's husband is no longer showing more of his feminine side, she will seek it from somewhere else. Of course, many sistas do not go to the extreme of straying to get the feminine energy from their man. Many sistas live by their taught morals-, which are so deeply ingrained that they do not realize that may want the energy of another man but refuse it because of what they have been taught.

Women are tired of the same old man shit, and they are gravitating to the brothas who are listening to them, who are rubbing them gently without having to have sex with them, who are doing the small things like rubbing their feet. Many brothas feel that as long as their woman is screaming when having an orgasm, then she is satisfied with the relationship. Brotha, it takes more than

The ScreamBed Chronicles

creamy thighs and paid bills to cultivate the relationship with your wife or girlfriend.

What is sad is that most brothas who are being played DO NOT EVEN KNOW. In their minds, they know everything about their woman, where she is, what 'girlfriends' she's at the play with. It turns out that them 'girlfriends' may look more like you- and may be in 'your pussy' making your woman scream in delight. She's at the play all right, you are the star and they're both watching you get played.

A woman, when she wants to fuck around, usually do it better than most men can. Because many men seldom take an interest in going to the bookstore, or to a play, in other words, doing things that many women enjoy. It is convenient for her to go under the auspices of hanging with the girls. Many women also can play a better role with her man when she is messing around than many men could, the sex may still come (unless of course, the other man is much better than her man is), and playasista may still profess her love for her man. She will maintain the role-playing for a while, until feelings get involved. When the other man is no longer just an outlet for her screaming pent-up feeling soul, which is when the trouble with her husband or boyfriend starts.

She will increase her times spent with

The PlayaSista underground

her 'girlfriends', sex with her boyfriend or husband may become almost non-existent and arguments may increase. Of course, this is very generic scenario of the signs of a straying woman, as some sistas will always invariably slip through the cracks, when analyzing them and their behaviors.

It is better to deal with this issue from the brotha end of it. If the men would address the issues that make it easier for women to stray, then it would become a smaller issue to deal with. Brothas should:

1) Explore and adore their own spiritual self as women are naturally tuned into spirit-relationships that have a spiritual foundation do much better than those that don't.

2) Cuddle with their woman in bed without always expecting sex

3) Rub her feet, her hands, her head, massage her, gently touch her, look into her eyes while telling her that he love her

4) Never take their women for granted, as it will backfire on them one day.

Many brothas who are major playas, usually have one thing in common, they were married to or dated at least one woman who I would refer to as the sista dog. In other

The ScreamBed Chronicles

words, she deals with men as the typical brotha who a dog is will deal with women. She loves men and her actions show it. Many of these men tried to do all the right things in the relationship, but the sista dog was above all that. She may feel that she genuinely loves her man, but she also feel that she could love more than one man- usually in a different way. Society frowns down on women who carry on in this way, unlike their male counterparts, who are treated like celebrities by the movie and television industries and society.
Women who are playas are greatly feared by most men, for they know deep down that when women play, they are master tricksters.

The women who love men too much, like their male counterparts are usually dealing with self-esteem issues. While a few are dealing with past sexual or other abuses during their childhood, many just love the chase with the accompanying fear inherent in straying and the sex. I've known sistas in the past from all of these levels and I got along with them, especially during my own playa days, I was careful that if I got involved with them on a more intimate level, I wouldn't allow my heart to slip into the abyss of unrequited love and possible heartbreak.

The PlayaSista underground

Straying is not as much a right or wrong issue as every soul has a purpose for being, everyone comes with some issue or issues that need to be worked out at some point in their development. Many mental professionals may argue that the issues should or is best worked out before the end of childhood. That may not be what that soul chose in its experience on this earth. The playa-sista may look at men as objects, maybe because she has realized that in the grand scheme of things, it's not about God looking down unfavorably on being a playa sista. The same could be said of relationships. Is their purpose deeper than just being committed to each other as we have been taught?

What if the issues of fidelity and trust are created only for our earth experience and for our soul's progression to a fearless, trustful, and jealous-free state of being?

I am not trying to advocate everyone having affairs and carrying on with others outside of their committed relationships. I am sure people wonder about the main issues that keep cropping up in divorce cases and other causes for breakups. Sexuality and affection is such a big part of our physical lives; that we must wonder if we are suppressing those parts of our self

The ScreamBed Chronicles

by committing ourselves in monogamous long-term relationships and marriages.

What if the idea of marriage was something designed to only protect man's ego, self-esteem and property values as suggested by researching history, especially religious history? I agree with many that it would not be wise to advocate that couples start having affairs; I only advocate the idea of a spiritual union. A marriage does not automatically make a spiritual union. At the basic level, a marriage is a governmental union that may or may not be witnessed in a religious building. IT'S UP TO THE MARRIED OR COMMITTED TO SPIRITUALLY BOND WITH EACH OTHER. Brothas who are hurt by the playa-sistas need to acknowledge their hurt and move on, just as the sistas who are hurt by the guys in their past. The hurt brotha may need more therapy, because of the size of my guys egos. Most men are never prepared for the hurt feelings they experience in dealing with the playa-sista.

I thought u were mine

I showed u the other side of the world
I just knew u were mine
always felt your love inside
girl, I didn't know that u could hurt me
I showed your heart a sort of purity
but u were looking at him
mind, body, soul, and there was no unity
u were looking at him
I thought u were mine
loving me so blind
Different woman
I'll pull out my hair
If u say he's not in your heart
Different woman
I'll promise not to stare
if we can have another start
I showed u what it is to love
and the meaning of God and all
u kicked me up the street
Girl I just wanna kiss u
before u go into the blue
I thought u were mine
loving me so blind
Different woman
I'll pull out my hair
If u say he's not in your heart
Different woman
I'll promise not to stare
if we can have another start

The ScreamBed Chronicles

Empty heart woman

Dear woman
Your eyes fool me
U've been hiding behind
A blue state of mind
Dear woman
Your heart's seeking
Energy that's
Not a part of me   .
Is it possible?
to see me as u see me
Or see me as u want me to be
There's no denying
That our wall keeps rising
Maintaining the outside
Without cleansing the inside
Woman, what u bring to me
Are things that I couldn't see
Woman-transform your mind
U'll see your reflection in me
Sweet woman
Your reality, may not be
It's all about what u put
in your mind, what u'll see with your eyes
Dear woman, I have love for u
Wanna see u thru
Dear woman I have love for u
Wanna see u thru
Woman, what u bring to me
are things that I couldn't see
Woman-transform your mind

The ScreamBed Chronicles

U'll see your reflection in me

Loser: Get the fuck on

Sistas, the task of identifying and avoiding guys that are playas or act like playas, shouldn't be too complicated. Instead, many women are not listening to their inner selves; they have lost much of their connection to the world of spirit and intuition. The 'going with the gut feeling' is systematically thrown out the window in favor of 'letting things go with the flow', or 'maybe he'll change with time'.

When you are in a relationship and something does not feel quite right about your boyfriend or husband, then you should simply ask God what's the deal with him? Listen for an answer that's not coming from a mind that wants the relationship to last,

The ScreamBed Chronicles

but listen with an objective mind, that's also not being overly negative towards your man. You only want an answer. Remember sista, being woman, you are already naturally more intuitive, so when you get that 'feeling' that your man may be 'squirting his shit' in another woman, then you should have a frank discussion with him about your concerns.

The above advice is for the women who are dealing with the pros, fortunately the fake playas and 'phony pimps' are much easier to root out. Sistas, you know these men all too well. They get the late calls with the accompanying secretive sounding, whispering voices. They are always hanging with 'the boys' and sometimes the other woman will somehow get your number and call you to tell you the deal with her and 'your man'. Lose his ass.

Nowadays, sistas have other types of deception to deal with: their men fucking men. These are the so- called, down low brothas. A few years back, I met a young brotha from another country who used to work in a mall in which a female friend and I ate lunch almost daily. This guy was around 19 or 20 at the time, silly, outgoing, and friendly. A year had passed since we saw our friend. Then one day, heading to our favorite table, a strange woman came up to us in a half

Loser: Get the fuck on

flirting way. She said, "Don't act like you don't know me." Now my lunch friend is NOT the one to talk crazy like this to, especially when she's about to put some food into her mouth.

After a minute, or so, of playing the guessing game, my friend starts telling this woman about the need to be respectful, and letting her know that we don't know her and asked her to leave our table. The woman then asked us if we remembered the little guy from so and so restaurant in the mall. We told her yes. She then shrugged her shoulders as if to say, I am the little guy. My friend and I looked at each other in disbelief, saying "hell no!" at almost the same time. Looking at this 'woman/man' with cocked eyes and angled heads, the guy had become a woman. Being in Atlanta, that is not a major surprise, but to have known the guy in his 'pre-girl' state was too much for my friend. She politely told the guy, "We need to eat now, so see you later."

Since then, I have run into this guy a few times on the street. One night, while walking down Peachtree Street, coming from the drugstore, I noticed far ahead, a woman was walking towards me. As I got closer, I realized that this 'woman' was the guy from the mall. I spoke to him, asking him what he was doing out here (as this section of

The ScreamBed Chronicles

Peachtree is known for transvestite prostitutes).

He says that he is picking up men for money because he must pay his rent. Starting to feel like a journalist, I wanted to know what type of guys he tricked. He said, "I only fuck straight guys!" Of course, I seized the few words that would seemingly shoot his statement down, "How can you call them guys straight when they're fucking with you, a man?" He nonchalantly replied, "These niggas appear as straight men to society, they have wives and girlfriends. I only fuck with men that have wives or girlfriends!"

Wow! I left with an uneasy feeling in my stomach, saying bye to him and to be careful out there on the streets. I do not have issues with people choosing to be with the same sex (if that is their thing), my main issue is if a man has a girlfriend or wife, and he wants to have a double life (especially with another man), then he should respect his woman and let his intentions be known. It's only fair and he's truly being a man. Give the sista a chance to decide if that is what she wants. I can understand why brothas would be secretive but being a real man will involve standing up for what you believe. If a guy is feeling the act of putting his dick in a man's ass or mouth, then stand up for it, be a man!

Loser: Get the fuck on

Sure, he may be talked about, misunderstood, banned from his parent's house or church. Nevertheless, he should be a man and stand up for what he likes! The 'down low movement' is becoming a bigger visible trend in young and older black men, but at least it's coming out and women are more aware of these kinds of bisexual men. Yes, I said BISEXUAL men, when a man sleeps with a woman and a MAN, this is BISEXUALITY. Although many down low guys think that they're straight because they only do the doing (a top), rather than being fucked (a bottom). Some of them even think that giving or receiving 'head' will keep them in the straight category. Sorry guys, you are bisexual! The earlier words regarding guys being respectful to their women and giving them a choice, are not just reserved for the 'straight' brothas, who happen to fuck men; this applies to the brothas who fuck around with other women too. Herpes, Chlamydia, gonorrhea, and syphilis are serious guests to bring home, and they cross the gender boundaries, not caring about whether you are gay, bisexual, or straight.

It's time for more straight talk: if your man is always hounding you about ass fucking, then you need to be a little concerned about where he likes to put his dick. Before all the freaks start calling me a

The ScreamBed Chronicles

prude, I am not saying that all men who like to ass-fuck their women are possibly fucking with men, but not too many truly straight men, will harass women about ass fucking them, when a vagina is so much easier to penetrate. Also, if your man wants to do some 'salad tossing' or eating ass, you might be a little concerned about that also. Again, there are a few straight men that may enjoy doing this, but the operative word is few.

My theory is that most of the down low brothas want to tell somebody their secret, but only in small doses. They're showing you their true desires with the incessant ass fucking and asshole licking. Sistas, identify the signs of a straying man! Most men are not trying to hang with the boys all the time, unless either he is fucking the boys, fucking another woman, or he just does not like you enough to want to be around you!

You can do fine by yourself until you meet the right guy. Many women are all caught up in the emotions and it is much harder to shake the playa out of the relationship that is when it takes a lot of patience and discipline. Say to yourself, 'I would rather be unhappy for a minute than be unhappy for a lifetime'. Women need to demand respect. If the man does not love

Loser: Get the fuck on

you right now, at the minimum, he should respect you.

This is the anti playa game plan:

1. Any man that refers to women (especially women who are strong minded and opinionated) as bitches or ho's, do not need to get as far as getting your number!
Any man that tries to force himself on you (as in having sex) and then gets an attitude or disappears for a minute, don't deserve to smell your vagina, much less put his penis in it!

2. Any man that cannot take you to a park, cultural function, concert, or a restaurant (other than a fast food place), does not deserve you; you are way too high class for his ass!

3. If a man constantly talks about his past, girlfriends as if he is bragging about the things that he got away with while in that relationship, well sista if you do not dump his ass, then you are not too bright!

There is NO man that is worth any potential heartache, you simply DESERVE better! You are a goddess, a queen and to be treated any less than that, you are missing a lot in life. Avoid the playa, pimp, and loser; tell them to GET THE FUCK ON!

The ScreamBed Chronicles

Brotha ho season

When my second wife and I decided to separate a few years back, I was not

thinking about going back to being a dog and fucking around with many women, I figured that we would be separated at most for two to three weeks. As three weeks rolled around, my wife wanted to know when I was coming home, I told her that I was not ready. After about a month, I realized that there were too many issues between us that a separation was not going to address properly. So after another month of thinking things through, I filed for

The ScreamBed Chronicles

divorce. Even currently, I was not thinking about the consequences of being single again; I just wanted the split to be smooth as possible for her and our child.

I had been faithful during the six years, my wife and I were together, and the thoughts of being single were a little unsettling. Questions came to me such as what would it be like to date different women and have sex with these women? After all, I had started feeling in the last couple of years in the marriage that I rushed this marriage after the first marriage ended. Maybe I was ready to go back to sowing my wild oats again. The more I thought about it, the more it seemed the cool thing to do. Then my rational side kicked in, reminding myself that even at the young age of 23 (when I married the first time), I was ready to settle down. So, I started thinking that maybe being a dog at age 36 wasn't as good an idea.

One particularly introspective day, I thought about my past marriages, past relationships, I realized that I brought things to the table in both marriages that contributed to their downfalls and eventually their end. I then prayed to the Great Spirit that ONLY the right woman would come into my life, for a future serious relationship, and if she were not the right woman, then the relationship would

Brotha ho season

not last or even get started. I had just started a new job two weeks after leaving my wife. After about a week at the new job, I met a sista there, that was not too shy about meeting me and wanting to get to know me. I thought about lying to her about my intentions (as she wanted to know if I had somebody, I told her no). She asked if I wanted to be in a relationship, I told her not now, but back in the day, I was good at manipulating sistas and lying to have sex with them. I thought about it briefly, but I knew this sista was serious about being in a relationship of some kind. If she saw through my bullshit, she could possibly try to challenge me or try giving me the beat down!

During this time, I was in a nearly all female band, which was good for me because the sistas were truly being my friends. They gave me a lot of good advice regarding my marriage before we split. They were NOT being impartial to me either. They sided with my wife many more times, than even she had realized. But, back to my work friend, after feeling like I was being interviewed for a position as her potential boyfriend, I would play back my band members' mantra to me after my split: "you don't need to get into a serious anything right now, you need to have some time

The ScreamBed Chronicles

alone." I also realized (based on my analysis of her personality) that New Job-sista and I would not be good for each other in anything serious, so we eventually became friends. A few months later, after a wine fueled and 'spaced out brownie' session at a party, I was hit on by a sista that I had known for almost a year. I had been trying to holla at a few sistas at the party; she 'pulled' me into a room, letting me know of her dissatisfaction with my actions (I was also close to capturing her friend as well).

Telling me that she wanted to be my girl (of course I realized that the wine and space brownies were doing most of the talking). Later that night, I 'rushed my high' to be able to hook up with her. We ended up at my spot, after what seemed to be an hour or so of driving around the city. We were fucked up and horny, we later fucked until we both fell asleep on each other.

Later that morning, upon awakening, she 'acted like she was innocent and didn't know what was up'. We fucked some more. This affair (she had a boyfriend and I was still legally married) only lasted for a couple of months. I enjoyed it and briefly entertained the idea of being with her in a more serious relationship. I heard the echoes of my being by myself mantra; we

Brotha ho season

both agreed that we needed to operate under the radar, because of our situations. The sex was good, though she was a bit of a wild girl type: she fast-forwarded me to the present, showing me how the dating landscape had changed since I was younger.

Enter woman number two; I met her during a concert at a small Atlanta nightspot. She and I had been exchanging quick glances at one another in the earlier part of the night. She had a somewhat exotic look about her. When the concert starts, I look to my right and see her standing there, smiling. She makes some small talk and by the second song, we're exchanging numbers.

A few days afterwards, I met this attractive older sista. When I met her, I felt her energy towards me. I could tell by her demeanor that she was a little older than I was, but she was pretty and had a nice body. We eventually got in touch with each other through a mutual friend and I invited her over one night. She came by during 'booty call' hours. I was extremely nervous for whatever reason, as she was sweating me hard. I had no reason to be nervous. My mind starts racing, "What if I don't please her sexually?" We fucked and it was...okay, I do not think I rated any higher than that with her either. We did not call each other afterwards.

The ScreamBed Chronicles

Back to woman number two, within a couple of weeks, we're having sex and a couple of months later, we're now 'involved'. The relationship was a hectic, fast moving 'situation'. After a couple of months of calling each other girlfriend and boyfriend, I broke it off. I liked her in some ways, but there were other things about her that I did not like, this was a case of 'If only she...' Before I broke up with number two, I met woman number three via email, through a mutual friend of ours. We had a few things in common like similar tastes in music and fashion sense. I liked her personality much better, than number two, but upon meeting her, she did not really move me with her style. She did not have flavor like the previous sista. We had sex a week after we met in person. It was good; she loved to have sex, as she had been celibate for about two years.

We eventually started calling each other 'girlfriend and boyfriend' after a month, but the relationship fizzled after about two more months. Neither of us really ended it, it just fell apart. I started questioning whether I could be in a successful relationship, after burning through two sistas in less than five months.

Brotha ho season

I met a younger sista at a natural foods store (she worked there) probably a week or so afterwards. The first day I saw her, we both locked eyes. She was hot, had a nice booty, cute face, and nice exotic hair. After doing a little background investigating, I introduced myself, and gave her my number and told her that she can call me when she gets the time. She gave me her number, saying that she was somewhat busy during this period, but she will have some free time in a week. I am nervous.

Again-this woman is sweating me, she is young, and so why am I nervous? I did not call her until a few weeks later. We kept missing each other, so I put her on the back burner. I saw her several weeks later and she asked me to call her. I called her a week or so later. She told me that she might be able to come by later that night. I waited a few hours, no call from her. She ended up calling all right...at 12:30 midnight. She was ready to come by, so I picked her up around 1:30am on a work night.

I knew this pick up was well into 'booty call' territory, but something happened to me. I felt that I should get to know her through conversing with her. This is not my old self in action! Even though she was hinting about wanting to have sex, I denied her flirtations, refusing to even make out with her. I had a flood of

The ScreamBed Chronicles

thoughts, wondering if she would refuse if I made my move. What if she is thinking that I am gay because I'm not making a move? She is a young sista and she looks quite like the innocent looking freak. Still I made no move. After about an hour of no action, she seems like she is a mixture of disappointment and disgust ("I'm fine, why this nigga ain't trying to hit it?") She asked to be taken home, on the way she did not say a word. I realized at that moment that I fucked it up with her. It was because of me. I had it in the bag. She hardly acknowledged me when I would shop in her store, I tried to make a bad situation better by calling her, and she never returned my calls.

One day during lunch, I ran into an old friend, who I had not seen in a few years. We spoke by phone often for a few weeks, then I invited her over, we hung out a little in my neighborhood. Later that night, we talked, both of us admitting our mutual attraction to each other in the past when we were in relationships. A few moments later, we were kissing and caressing each other. She had some reservations about going further. I convinced her to 'explore that which is your deepest urge unrealized'. She felt more comfortable a few minutes later and we had some good sex.

Brotha ho season

This relationship bordered on a more serious type of union. We both really liked each other. After a few more times having some hot sex, I started to feel that she was gently pulling away from me emotionally. Though her reasons were quite vague and 'mystical', I slowly realized that this woman was protecting her heart, sanity and she knew that financially, I was not ready for a relationship. Though she was feeling me, she was prophetic enough to know that though we were close in age, I would probably outgrow her as she was much more settled than I was. We continued to do things together and talk on the phone, strengthening our friendship.

During this time, I was laid off my job, but I was not officially told until a full month after this. I was bored out of my ass! I started looking for jobs online and decided to check out the online dating services. Online dating! My perception about this type of dating was not the best at one time, besides my ego would not lump me in the 'desperate category' which is what I felt people were if they dated online. After a few days of being a little hesitant and shy, I jumped headfirst in it.

I got a few replies after posting my generic picture on all the sites. I met a hot woman on one of the predominately black dating sites. Eventually, she got in

The ScreamBed Chronicles

touch with me by phone, came by after a week or so and we had some good sex. I was surprised a little when she did not call me afterwards, I am thinking to myself, the new dating age! I eventually called her, and she let me know that our sexual experience was nothing more than that... our meeting was only about sex and that is all she wanted!

The next couple of weeks, I met a couple of sistas over the internet. One woman caught my attention. On the first night of our online meeting, we exchanged telephone numbers and later, I called her. We had good conversation, never running out of things to talk about. We talked for five hours that night. When she came to visit me, I just knew that I was going to have her for dinner. Well, she seemed to have insecurity issues, and seemed to be playing games. A little insecurity is popping in. At this point in my dating life, I was probably at the lowest point in my self-esteem.

This sista helped to bring me closer to earth as far as my ego was concerned. After seeing her twice (we did not do anything but hug), she did not return my calls. I started telling some of my friends as well as myself that I only wanted sex and no relationship (I was only fooling my friends). I started to feel that I could not meet any interesting

Brotha ho season

sistas. The sistas that were trying to holla at me were usually between the ages of 19 and 25. I started to feel that maybe I do not appeal to women in my age group because of my sometimes abstract, eclectic style or maybe because they knew that I was unemployed.

I met another sista. She was older than I. We met on a Wednesday, she came by on the following Friday, and we fucked. She wanted to spend the night, but I remembered that one of my other sista friends was coming by early the next morning (along with more potential sex); I did not want an uneasy situation to manifest. Miss Friday really enjoyed sex and she was forthcoming about the nature of our relationship: she had been married a couple of times and she was not trying to find a man.

Those words were like gold to my ears, finally the perfect woman, someone I can fuck and not feel obligated to! But it didn't stay that way...I started to feel like I was obligated to come see her, to answer my cell phone when she called. She would question why I would not come visit her until late. After a few uneasy episodes with her, weeks later, I decided that perhaps she was really lying about what she wanted; that she really wanted a serious relationship but was acting as if she did not. Tensions

The ScreamBed Chronicles

between us rose a little, until we fizzled out. A week later, I seduced a sista whom I had worked with earlier in the year. I knew that she was attracted to me, I was not overly attracted to her at first, but she was attractive, I secretly felt that she was sexy. We ended up meeting at my spot one night, working on some music; after about thirty minutes of talking about music, I made my move. It started with me giving her a massage. When I got down to her big ass, my dick got hard as a brick and I started humping on her ass. I flipped her over, and we fucked. She spent the night. We had a few more fucking 'episodes' throughout the end of the year, culminating in a hot and horny night around the New Year.

Earlier in that 'last time' night, she claimed that she did not want to have any more sex. Though she was as horny as I was, she felt that sex was a waste when no one was trying to start a serious committed relationship (mainly me). Well, we ended up having the best sex since we began having sex. We fucked all night until it was time to get up.

A few weeks after fucking my former co-worker, I fucked another former co-worker. She too like the first one, was sexy, but not someone who I would have been attracted to particularly. We fucked only one time and it

Brotha ho season

was good. She wanted a repeat performance; I decided that it was best to keep it a single performance. I later, met a sista originally from Europe online, after conversing over the phone for a few days; we met at her place, during booty call hours. While she was not super attractive to me, she exuded an intense sexiness. We fucked on the first night of our meeting. It was good. We had good conversations and we had more good sex, but I knew that she was not a 'final stop' for me.

Each day, I got more frustrated about my joblessness and the Atlanta dating scene, one day I was talking to a platonic sista friend that was moving to New York, she told me directly that I should come up with her. "What about my children, they'll miss me, where are we going to live?" She shot back with some compelling reasons why I should go, "You don't have a job, you can visit your children, they can visit you, the girls in New York are hot, and they're not as into brothas having a lot of money or status as the Atlanta women are".

After a few days of scratching my head over this decision, I decided that I too, should move to New York. I started planning for my move, setting my job searches for NYC, looking for housing and setting my personals ads to NYC. I did see many jobs that I was qualified for with

The ScreamBed Chronicles

decent pay and I started applying. My
personals responses increased, so of course
my excitement for moving there increased.
Of course, the forces of rationality did not
allow me to move to New York, (it mainly
involved my asking the Great Spirit and
Angels for a sign whether I was going or
not). I went to visit my family in Augusta
for the Thanksgiving holidays, intending
only to stay for THAT holiday weekend, but
eventually staying on through early
January. I changed my dating profiles to
Augusta and that is where the fun begins!
The first couple of nights there, I met this
fine sista online. We instant messaged each
other for seven hours! Though we met a few
times in person, we never got any closer
than a hug at her job. I met a really fine,
younger sista online, we called each other a
few times, eventually meeting and going to
a couple of movies. She rode with me on one
of my many Augusta to Atlanta trips and
spent the night at my spot, we slept
partially nude, but we did not have sex! She
softly claimed that she was coming off her
cycle and that she was also 'trying' to be
celibate, I did not press it on.

A few days later, I met an older sista that
I eventually found to be too insecure for
me; we just 'played around' a bit. She was
pretty, had a juicy ass, and was horny. We

Brotha ho season

only dry humped, me spreading her legs in her living room on a lounger type chair, while hoping that her young son would not pop up in the room. While in my pants, I laid my hard dick near her pussy and grinded on her until she started pulling my hair and grimacing: she had an orgasm! After that, I did not hear from her and I did not call her.

I met a couple of women in South Carolina. One of them was ok, I was not too impressed with her real life looks, the other one was decent, we fucked the first and only day that I saw her. It was damn good! I contemplated on bringing her down to Atlanta, but eventually she faded out of my mental.

Later, I met a white woman online in Augusta; she was cool, cute, slim, and had a nice ass. We eventually met a week later at her place, though we did not have sex, we fucked a few days later. The sex was good, and I felt that she wanted me to stay overnight; I could not, because the young sista (who I secretly desired) was coming by early the next morning. After a few more times in bed with my earlier European woman friend, I realized that not only were we not compatible as a potential couple, I felt that I was settling by being with her.

The ScreamBed Chronicles

Knowing that she was starting to like me, I knew that I was not going there with her. During the whole time that I was in Augusta, I was fucking a woman that was close to my family at the time, who I had also known since high school. We never did anything back then other than grind on each other a little. It all started on Thanksgiving eve, she was helping prepare food, and during a brief period when we were alone, I started flirting with her. After noticing her body and especially the way that her ass filled her jeans, I got instantly aroused. I came up behind her, whispering in her ear about wanting her. She blushed and I kissed her on the neck. She jumped from the arousal and turned around to grab me and kiss me back. We made plans to hook up later in the back room that night.

She cracked the door open. I am in my boxers, with a hard dick and fast beating heart; I went straight to her wide-open thick thighs and waiting pussy. That was some of the best sex that I'd had in years, maybe it was because of the relative taboo nature of fucking her in my mom's house and doing it to someone-who I have always wanted to fuck. We fucked an average of three or four times a week during most of my stay in Augusta. The sex was satisfying and when she came, she came hard. One late night after getting in from Atlanta, I

Brotha ho season

fell asleep, at about four in the morning; my sister awakened me from a deep sleep, pointing in the direction of another bedroom. I groggily walked to the next room to find my fuck buddy waiting for me on the futon! She wanted to be served! That felt a little uneasy with me, as I did not want my sister to know about us. My fuck buddy was cool, she didn't have any drama.

By early January, I was officially back in Atlanta. I had gotten a promising job lead and I started looking back on my life during the last several months of unemployment. I admitted to myself that I really did not want a life of fucking different women anymore. I knew that I was running from the real reason that I was sexually involved with so many women in such a short time: I desired something more substantial in a relationship. I would manage to fool others with my lies of not wanting a serious relationship, but I could not fool myself. The single life was not what I imagined it would have been.

Today's women were not the girls of yesteryear, the ones that literally would fall at my feet just to give me what I wanted. I was in a new world, a world where looks were not the only barometer that women measured men by. Feelings of insecurity crept in briefly: what if I'm too slim, maybe I need to make good money, or I need a job.

The ScreamBed Chronicles

For the first time in my life, I felt like a washed up old playa. Though I was sexually involved with a few women during the last few months, I still felt empty inside. Besides, these women were on the outer edges of what I wanted to be with, they were fulfilling a need, albeit a selfish need of mine. I felt that maybe the Universe was finally punishing me for my past misdeeds (broken marriages, playing with old girlfriends' hearts).

One night, after praying and meditating, I remembered the prayer that I did around the time I left my last wife. "Only the right woman will come into my life." That's it! I am not some has-been; I have simply not met the right woman yet. At this point, I decided to become celibate, as I needed to cleanse my mind, body, and soul of the overt sexual energy from the past few months.

I figured that I would sexually fast for a month. It eventually lasted for nearly four months. I felt good during my celibacy period. I started a new job, joined a cool band, and moved in with a cool sista (no I did not try to fuck her). I started looking at women in another light. Though I had gone through several women enlightening periods in the past, I could feel a higher level of respect towards women.

Brotha ho season

This celibacy period made me re-evaluate my relationships with all the women in my past. I felt much remorse for how I treated my past wives and some girlfriends. I made a new commitment to myself that the next woman in my life would reap the rewards of this enlightenment. She would have a man that is committed 200 percent to making things work, being considerate, and being more loving. This new woman would have my full attention.

I give thanks to my knowing that I needed to be celibate, so that the stage would be prepared for this special woman's entrance into my life. This special woman did come into my life. She is like all the best aspects of most of my relationships in the past rolled into one. Though I met her over a year before we got involved, I know that without my recent fuck-fest and subsequent celibacy, I probably would have come off wrong towards her and she would have seen through me instantly. I can honestly say that I love her, I respect her, I cherish her, and I want her to be in my life forever!

My past relationships prepared me for my present relationship, so I do not have any regrets about ANY of my past relationships as they had to be what they were for the experiences. My two marriages forced me to grow up: even my experiences in the bands

The ScreamBed Chronicles

had an influence in creating a kinder, gentler, more loving self. During the nearly two-year journey from married man to boyfriend, then to Brotha Ho, I truly cracked open my subconscious mind, peeling off layers of denial, hurt and lost love to find my true self. This self had been covered since I decided that I wanted to settle down as a 23-year-old. I was searching for my true self and I found it through experiencing ALL the beautiful women that I had in my life. What many brothas do not realize is that sistas will make you strong, it is in their nature, and they cannot help it! They will force the real man to manifest. It is a process though, a process that is aided by a downsized male ego that will allow his woman to assist in his growth.

When the girls go out

This essay highlights women

who are either current playas or former playas. I have used names of their choosing to protect the not so innocent as well as keep their playmates and played husbands or boyfriends out of my freaking hair as well as my name out of their lawsuits. These are real sistas fucking around on real guys with real guys, this section was not written to judge anyone's activities, but to show the guys who don't know; that women do fuck around and they do it better than most guys do. So brothas, watch your backs... when the girls go out!

The ScreamBed Chronicles

Red

My first interviewee is a tall, very shapely Amazonian who I will call Red. Red is mostly a playa, but she does not like the term. "Playas use people to get money or material things; I just like to play with their body, not their pocket. Red's term for men is 'toys'. Maybe one of the reasons why men are referred to as toys is because Red mostly attracts and 'plays' with men younger than herself. Red is in her fifties.

"One of my most memorable sexual encounters was with this 26-year-old perfectly hung guy. Overall, the sex was not bad, he just could not keep up with me, and I wore him out. He was begging me to stop, I told him to shut up and lay there so I could keep riding him. After much begging for me to stop, I told him he had to leave as he was there only to satisfy my needs."

Red does not like "one minute men" and she says no to "short dick" men, in fact she even has a mantra to keep small-endowed men away: "If it's not seven inches or more, don't even look in my door". "If I'm in a non-committed relationship, it's a good possibility that I will screw around." "I really like a man to give me affection, attention and of course, good sex. I have more of a male philosophy when it comes to sex. My libido is insatiable as I've only had

When the girls go out

four orgasms in my life, the rest of my
sexual encounters just felt good, I wanted
to climax so bad."

I asked Red if she was freaky in her
choice of place when having sex: "I'm not
much of a freak; I've only screwed on the
side of the road, in office parking garages
and on the beaches in the Bahamas and
Miami". Red however is outspoken when it
comes to the sexual encounter itself: "if it
doesn't feel good, I will stop it right there.
I'll only give a man two chances to screw me
right after the second chance, he won't have
another chance."

Red have been told by several lovers
that she is cold blooded and heartless. She
knows what she wants, and she does not
believe in pretending. She feels that many
women want to have sex, if not on the first
day of meeting a man-in the early days of
meeting him. "I believe in screwing the first
time I meet a guy. If some men are
immature and cannot handle that, then I
cannot be bothered. I consider men who call
women names such as slut, loose and
whorish as being sexually insecure. I have
had as many as five different guys in one
week, what's wrong with that? I have an
appetite!" Aesthetically, what type of guy
attracts Red? "I like very athletic looking
guys and after I turned 35 years old, it
seems that only younger guys were

The ScreamBed Chronicles

attracted to me. Maybe because I looked much younger than my age, I was not as attracted to older guys because many of them had pot-bellies, and that doesn't look good. I did have an encounter with a 43-year-old that came close to satisfying my sexual needs, but he is married, and I could not get him when I wanted him. It was like fireworks when we got together".

Red does not believe in men lying to get sex, like some men telling her that they love her when they do not or that they want to marry her when they will not. She says the man would get farther with her by giving her a choice on what she wants out of him. In her words, "honesty is a true aphrodisiac." Going back to married men, Red has been with a few married men, "it's not as fun because of their availability and excuses." She says that she really doesn't like to "deal" with another woman's headache, but in the same sentence will say that people can't control their physical attraction towards one another-whether they're married or not. "If I don't know their wife, then he's fair game, but if I do-then he's hands off for me." "I think that women should be more open about their sexuality and stop hiding behind old cultural taboos." Red offers a lesson to those women (beautiful and otherwise) who do not seem to attract men: "several years ago, I read a

When the girls go out

book about this unattractive woman who could attract many men. The woman would go into an office and the men there would swarm around her, she would walk in the mall, same thing. Even when she would go into a building, where there were beautiful women, she would attract more men than even the fine women. What was her secret? Sexuality. She oozed sexuality around her. The difference with her and many women that look sexy was that she was sexually secure with herself. That somehow was conveyed into the air around her and evidently it attracted the men." When asked how many women she would estimate thinks similarly to her, her reply: "a very small percentage because this is a cultural taboo and because their religions forbid it."

Delilah

The next sista, I will call Delilah. Delilah is successful in her career, highly intelligent, humorous and by all appearances, happily married. What many of her associates do not realize is that she put on a show when it comes to the 'happily married part'. Delilah is quick to point out to anyone in her 'inner secret circle', that she loves her husband dearly; but she feel that she's

The ScreamBed Chronicles

capable of loving more than one man on different levels at the same time. She says that she has never been played, but she has played every man she has been with including her husband. I asked her how she felt about her playing all her men, she replied in a matter of fact tone: "fine". "Playing around is the most natural thing. It must happen. I enjoy it. It works for me. Most people were not made for monogamy. A monogamous state is an unreal state and I think that each of us defines monogamy differently".

Delilah has been in a two, plus year, emotional affair with an out of town ex boyfriend. Almost every time she would see him, they would screw. If her boyfriend lived out of town, it was cool for Delilah, but when he started making marital overtures, asking her to move in with him; her feelings toward him started to change. "If I were to marry this clown, eventually I would find another man to mess around with".

Unlike Red earlier, Delilah's passions are not fueled as much by sex. While she is lost, on a man that is well hung and knowing how to swing it in bed, she loves the chase. That is- men chasing her. She likes the words that the most romantic of her men use to try to capture her fancy. Delilah does not believe in messing around

When the girls go out

with married men. "I want him to spend time with me when I want him to". Her 'moral' reason is "I wouldn't want a woman messing around with my husband". Although Delilah appears to be contradictory in her feelings about married men, when talking to her, she has her own theories on men, women, relationships, and all the glue that binds it all together.

Ebony

Ebony was not a conscious playa, only realizing what she did after she got older. "I didn't think about it, it was what I did; I say it now that I hurt guys. I did not take the time to think about how I affected the guys; because it was a guy, I assumed it was all right. My former boyfriend expressed his hurt from a while back."

Sex was introduced to Ebony in a most vicious way: her father raped her at the age of 13. "I can't stand being emotionally hurt by a man". Ebony is a living contradiction; she was raised with old school values, having never kissed a boy before the age of 13. She could not even go outside until she was older. When she was 15, she got pregnant by a 19-year-old man, who denied it was his. Still, it took prodding from her

The Screambed Chronicles

mother for her to realize that she was pregnant. She got the first of four abortions, between the ages of 15 and 21, with the bulk of them happening between 19 and 21, her most promiscuous phase. "In many situations, I didn't want to do this (have sex) but would let it happen anyway."

When she was 19, she started dancing at an Atlanta strip club; eventually she started screwing the owner of the club. One night, she met this guy at a popular nightspot, they talked, she gave him her number, he showed up at her house and they kicked it until the early morning. "One night the guy picked me up, we ended up at a motel, I was high, we screwed, and at three in the morning, I awoke wondering how I got here and he was gone." Usually, it's the guy that would get the ill treatment, after having sex". Ebony would kick him out the door. She maintains that she has never been broken hearted though and she feels like she is opening a bit emotionally.

"Three fourths of all my sexual encounters at the time, I didn't want to do, being that I hadn't dealt emotionally with my rape at 13 yet, I was more worried about what the guys would think if I said no, putting their feelings ahead of mine. After many of the sexual encounters, I felt mentally raped (remembering that she said no to her father before the first time he raped her) she felt

When the girls go out

saying no to these guys would get the same result (that they would take it)." She has been in an on off relationship with a certain guy since she was 18. "Whenever we would break up and if he started seeing someone, I would stalk him." Ebony admits that having sex was a much easier way for her to communicate with guys, rather than talking and opening up emotionally.

"Right now, I'm domesticated, I've already done it all, I've stolen, ran the streets, as far as the present, cheating wouldn't be an option now, it doesn't get me anywhere." Recently, she met a guy that she's really feeling, but she's afraid to open up emotionally, worrying what he might say or think about her. She has been very emotional about this guy.

Soultrane

Soultrane started the boy/ dating thing later than many girls did, when she was 18 years old, kissing her first time at 16. Between the ages of 19-21, she found herself not only in her first real relationship but torn between two guys. The first of the two guys 'taught' her the playa game. Her next relationship was between the ages 22-26 dating the same guy. However, Soultrane got a little greedy.

The ScreamBed Chronicles

she met this 19-year-old guy at her job and started a mental and emotional affair. This happened after about a year into the relationship. She and the main man were living together and after a while, she would leave home, travel 25 miles to see the other guy.

They did not have sex for a while, and when they did, she says it was "just because" and not because there was a shortage of good sex at home. She felt that it was natural for them to go there. Her new 'friend' was more available, and they would have more sex, of course, feelings got involved. To take the heat off her guilty feelings, she would mentally blame him for her playa ways, even starting discussions with her boyfriend that would allow her to transfer her anger about her "situation" onto him. Despite all the developing drama, he was not too inquisitive about her whereabouts. More feelings came. Later, she did not want to go home, hating that she lived with her boyfriend, regretting that she cannot bring her new friend over and splash around in her bed. She later decided not to shack up with anyone else.

When the girls go out

The affair ended after her boyfriend got into an accident, he ended up getting home before her, when she got in, and he had many questions about the where's, what's and who is of her being out so late. Then the other guy left the States, going back to St. Croix.

Soultrane's next 'playa incident' was with her next-door neighbor (she was with the same boyfriend). She is claiming that it is her boyfriend's fault, "because he hung out with the guy". Her boyfriend befriended the handsome new neighbor, whom she was attracted to from day one. Eventually, her boyfriend would confide to the neighbor, telling him his intentions of breaking up with Soultrane after he moves out. Of course, when her boyfriend moved out, she 'got closer' to the neighbor, and of course, the neighbor told her of the boyfriend's intentions. Perfect move...on the boyfriend's part, his running off at the mouth, only 'pushed' Soultrane into the arms of the neighbor.

She had an affair with the neighbor for about six months. It was something special about this neighbor guy, from day one, she felt like she was in a trance when she looked at him. "I never felt a connection with anyone else, like I did with him". She felt that even if her boyfriend had not made it easier to meet the neighbor guy, she

The ScreamBed Chronicles

would've 'dabbled' still. "Never had an instant attraction like that before".

Soultrane acknowledges that she seems to be more efficient in "work-related affairs" than any other is. She is in a two-year relationship now, they live together. She's found another willing participant in her playa game: a guy she was interested in when she didn't have a boyfriend. The guy eventually got married, and then later a divorce, her interest in him never subsided. Now unmarried, he is pursuing her, and she would consider this phase a mental affair. Soultrane invited this guy to her place two months after her boyfriend moved in. The boyfriend evidently trusts this 'friend' as he has had conversations with them, then left the two of them together several times. Soultrane says they have only kissed a few times when unattended to. How long will the innocence last?

Legs

Looking at Legs, one will have the perception of a confident sista who 'looks' like she can run things in a relationship but looking back on how Legs got started with guys, she wasn't always this confident. Her first sexual experience was around 16, recounting her earlier experiences, Legs says she was dumb, naïve

When the girls go out

and sex just was not good. She was also 16 when she got pregnant and had an abortion, this experience slowly opened her eyes about guys and their agendas. She was married in her mid twenties but stayed faithful to her husband.

After this marriage ended, she eventually met someone, getting into serious relationship. Legs realized that this relationship was not working, and she started seeing someone on the side.

She would use work and her sons' sporting activities as excuses to get out and do her thing. Her boyfriend did not ask questions and remembering her feelings during this period, she says, "it didn't feel right; it was out of my norm". She realized that she was not ready for a committed relationship, also eventually catching her boyfriend playing around. Shortly after catching him, they split up after three years together. Her next relationship saw her being faithful in the beginning, but she started messing around with a guy she rode home from work with. Her reasons: the boyfriend did not fulfill her sexually. Legs was very satisfied sexually with the new guy, but then she questioned whether she was truly satisfied, because sex was good or, she was bored with the relationship. She says that all her liaisons were mostly sexual.

The ScreamBed Chronicles

As Legs reached her mid 40's, she still had not found the man that could capture her fancy. She did meet an intellectual younger guy (in his late twenties), she describes this brotha as a cutie. They hit it off well after meeting in a local bar. They danced, talked, gazed into each other's eyes; he said all the right things. They were wrapped up into each other's conversation so much that they just had to "talk some more at his place". At his place, they walked around a romantic pathway outside at his apartment complex, holding hands and feeling much sexual tension between each other. They embraced, kissed, and they gazed into each other's eyes. Legs propped herself against a picnic table, slightly opening her miniskirted legs. They started grinding. He rubbed between her legs, feeling her pussy mound underneath wet panties; he gently pulled down her panties. Brotha man slid his hard dick into her hungry pussy. They fucked in the cool night air, not caring whether someone could walk up on them. They were in their moment.

Everything felt so right, though she does not usually give it up on the first night; this brotha seemed so right in many ways. The sex was good, and things seemed right, at least for a few weeks. Then things slowly

When the girls go out

changed, brotha man started acting as if he wanted to play a few games. Sometimes when Legs would visit him, he would be on his cell phone, talking in almost a hushed voice or going out to the balcony to talk, presumably with a female. Legs did not trip much about this, as they were NOT in a relationship much less a committed relationship. After he started questioning her about the calls she was getting, she would question him about his calls. His answers were ambiguous, as if he were trying to 'make her feel' a little insecure or jealous.

They would still hook up, have great sex, spend the night with each other, prepare each other breakfast and dinners, but they continued to question each other about other people. Legs slowly started pulling away from brotha man emotionally. When she eventually realized a few other things about him, she concluded that he was NOT ready for what she wanted a serious committed relationship. Obviously, he had a good many women in his past, but Legs soon realized that the women that he dealt with were probably more desperate then she could ever be. When he felt her pulling away, he then decided that he wanted to be around her most of the time. At this time, he also mysteriously 'lost' his female friends.

The ScreamBed Chronicles

Legs felt the urge to give him another chance, which she did. He started questioning her alot more about her phone calls and one day told her that she should not answer her own phone. Of course, Legs countered, "we're not in a relationship". Nevertheless, he could not explain why he did not want to explore the possibility of them being in a serious relationship. Legs felt that he was wasting her time. She pulled back again. He started calling her, asking her to 'hook up' with him. Legs did not go there with him, saying that she deserved better.

If brotha man could not get in touch with Legs, he would get stupid, blowing up both her job and cell phones. Sometimes she would not answer his calls everyday. Then he started getting stupider. He would call Legs, telling her that he needed the money back from her that he gave her or saying that he was hungry and had no money. She knew that he was acting out of being insecure and knowing that he fucked up his chance to be right with a hot sista. Over a period of a month, he kept up the calling, harassment, and damn near begging. One day when Legs arrived at work, she checked her voice mail and heard a pitiful voice. It was brotha man, but this time, instead of the braggart sounding voice

176

When the girls go out

that had been aggressively posturing to her. She heard the voice of a boy. Though this boy had grown into a man of his late twenties, he had not left the insecurities of his earlier years behind. Legs also had suspected for a few weeks, that Mr. 'I got game with many ho's', was crying his little pitiful eyes out about their 'situation'.

Well, this voice mail message confirmed that he was a 'fake ass playa'. Sounding as if he had been crying before calling her, Legs felt that he had been crying after thinking deeply about how things could have been, but now knowing that his own immaturity and bullshit turned Legs off; there was nothing that he could do about it. The voice mail also confirmed that he did not even have other women 'stacked up' as he alluded to. Legs even sarcastically asked him about his 'women' whereabouts.

This guy's example is a sad story. Sad because a young brotha, tried to play an older sista, but he was just a neophyte in the game. He did not do his homework; he had not counted on Legs being hip to his shit. He did not factor in the fact that while she may be single, Legs was NOT a desperate dame. Nevertheless, Legs is the kind of sista that is smart, she knows game, she is enlightened to a wide variety of subjects, and that she attracts many different types of guys. That combination is

The ScreamBed Chronicles

dangerous for the inexperienced so-called playa, that combination also makes Legs a man-eater.

Legs clearly got the most out of this short relationship. She got some good dick, and she played teacher to a 'wet behind the ears' 'boy' who hopefully learned that if he wants to run with the big dogs, he needs to remember his hurtful summer lesson with Legs.

California girl

I've been watching u
your new hair do's, funky clothes
But U actually scare me
there's something about U that can pull
me...into orbit
U can encourage me...with a swing of your
back end
To engage into something that will feel good
something that'll keep us coming.... coming
back for more
I've been watching u, though I talk to u, I
don't talk as much as I feel
Because u scare me...in the best way
When u walk, it's like motion poetry
When u talk, my mind drifts into a secret
imagination
Good imagination, where we explore our
tickle zones
Where I massage your head, u rub my back
i just wanna nibble your ear, your neck,
your big peach
before u think it's all about the physical
it's your thinking, the way u smile
u make me blush when I don't want to
u make me nervous when I try to be cool
rather than expose my secret lust crush, I'd
rather keep it hush
u scare me

The ScreamBed Chronicles

I secretly paint u with my essence in my
nightly thoughts
I could lose myself, inside u
Addicted is me after tasting u
U don't even know, my thoughts, my secret
passion

What do u like?

Who are u?
What do u like?
Do u like candle wax, dripping, dripping...?
What about honey painted around your....
on your...
U seem like u like being on top, positioning
your part to mine
A perfect fit, a perfect explosion
What if I slide it...in from the back...the
hump
Riding your big apple
Hitting spots that u couldn't do without the
buzzing thing
What do u feel?
Is it just right? Too small, too big
Stabbing u just right?
At this time...it's all about u
U should feel high, to compensate those
times
in the past when u were frustrated, orgasms
that were too shy
Guys that were too sleep and slack
Feel high
I wanna know
What do u like?

I tried math, but the banana exploded anyway

Your words slither around me
they're alive calling my name n the moment
wrapping   ourselves   into   a   thousand
screams
u move as a graceful dancer
horizontally trapping me in the box of "turn
out"
your words feed me ego sandwiches
grabbing me, impregnating my soul
love.... love....love
my toes, my heels, my stomach, chest
feeling your energy, in our cocoon
I must think about math now
To hold back, to stop the flow
It's getting harder to hold back
Your juicy melon, communicating with my
throbbing self
Ignoring its eventual explosion
Um...Geometry.....sine...cosine....taaangent

Apple juice

Your eyes they feed me
Notions
Walking past u...I blush
Ideas...feed me
Juicy tilapia and I'm ready
We want each other
I'm scared...of your big apple
 And what it means to take a bite
I'll want apple juice...your life
Where were u when I was one
Now, you're here and your legs
Tell me stories of intellect
And goooood apple juice.
My dreams feature u
in a perfect balance of mind
Soul and body
In the dream, I had u
Underneath...me
We danced n the covers
Then the ring of my clock
Bzzzzzzz
Wake me from the apple juice...

BrainDiary1: Danger and the platonic people

MAN
I have a friend, a most delightful one-year
friend
We hang out in bookstores, cafes, and the
occasional concert
We're both independently unattached
But lately, I've been feeling....
WOMAN
He's such a cool guy, we hang out
Maybe I'm like "one of the guys" to him
I never have to worry about him hitting on
me
In the beginning, I wondered if he might be
gay
That notion went up in flames, when....
MAN
Something is itching me, deep in my mind
About this woman, she wore something the
other day
That caught my manhood
This anxious feeling rose to the surface
WOMAN
He gave me his major eyes
After seeing me in my...fitting mini and
heels
I felt funny, and I had a heavy inside smile
I wonder what he...
MAN
People already think that we're bound
together

The ScreamBed Chronicles

It's how close we stand in the public space
Sometimes I catch her eyes, looking down
Anxious energy, center on my piece
Sizing her at the rear, the front, I feel light
WOMAN
Think I'll position myself, for a show
I feel a little anxious, thinking about his energy
Feelings can destroy a beautiful thing
If it's so good, I'll want more
Conflict of the highest
MAN
She's serving me her specialty, my friend
Possibilities of the evening creep into a hungry mind
She's got ambiance, I've got nerves, that won't calm
She's wearing another mini, with legs screaming out for me to caress
Hmmm....
WOMAN
My ass feels like it's on fire when I walk past him
Will he make a move? I smile with thoughts of him
Spreading me out, right now, with the carpet as our bed
Anxiousness is my close friend now
As I sit close...
MAN
Hornyness, replaces hunger as my friend
While gazing into her most beautiful eyes

BrainDiary1: Danger and the platonic people

I whisper I want u
She smiles, now anxiety goes away with a knowing...
WOMAN
He plants a kiss near the back of my neck
I feel a rush from my toes, up my back
He's dangerous and I feel like I want danger
Wetness is what I feel...
MAN
I catch her luscious lips, and our tongues dance like nasty teens
I nibble every part of her
Parts that she was unaware had *those* kinds of feelings
MAN AND WOMAN
We did things that the dark only knows
We felt things that our bodies and minds, can't seem to compare with our past
We were reborn that night
We cried and passed out
Our experience is the secret and the connection to our continued good friendship....

BrainDiary2: The continuation of the connection

MAN
I'm in the bed, thinking
Looking at the ceiling
I see her, dancing gracefully
My friend, but now, she's MY FRIEND
Can't get her out of my mind
Our connection...is getting stronger

WOMAN
I wonder what he's doing.... thinking
Can't get him out of my...head
When we merge, the memory can't escape
me
My body was aching for him...I didn't know

MAN
Passing her desk, my heart races, memories
of our nights make me stop
I can't help myself, looking into her eyes,
our knowing secret
Ideas are popping up...at the job
Where can I take her? I'm so feeling to be
inside of softness

WOMAN
Seeing him, is different...after he touched
me
I wanna rub him as he walks past my desk

The ScreamBed Chronicles

my thinking makes me like a juicy mango
there must be a place....
A special spot, cuddle spot

MAN AND WOMAN
We did the unthinkable...after finding a
barren, dark room
The room was the center of our silent
scream cinema
It felt good and felt scary.... her on me/ him
on me, in the twirling chair

Doing it like it's the last time ever
The sound of our muffled breaths and
slippery bodies, scream out of the stillness
Then, there's release....

BrainDiary3: Conflict brewing a new coffee hell

MAN AND WOMAN
We're flowing, still knowing
Our times in secret rooms
It keeps getting better, our loving

WOMAN
This other guy's starting to bother me
His questions dealing with intimacy
Whether my friend and I have gone there
His girlfriend works with us
Knowing nothing of his affections for me
But he had his chance.... right?

MAN
My love for my friend explodes red
Sometimes, I feel that something's missing
Like she's not telling me something
There's another energy around her
I long for more mango, juicy mango

WOMAN
Though there's nothing going on with us....
anymore
He's asking about my friend
Wanting to know what part of me have I
shared
None of your business-you girlfriend
wracked wreck

The ScreamBed Chronicles

He's....
ANOTHER MAN
Why and what do u see in this "man thing"
U know what I feel, my feelings I won't conceal
Giving this strange man your time and fruit
Remember our times, the parking garage, u releasing 3 times
I miss u, I want u
I dream u and our passion
I hear u and your screams
Let's do our thing
Forget his strangeness, he's a punk

Brain Diary4: Comeback of the twista and the eventual elimination

OTHER MAN:
Gotta have more of u, a little some at least
While making love to my girl, on a hot moon night
I was thinking of u, our times, and twists.
Gotta have u, be in u....

WOMAN:
Your chance was in your lap, a few seasons back
But remember, your girl that u wanted to respect
The one with the arrow at your heart
I don't remember when u crossed my mind....

OTHER MAN:
Your legs, I must kiss...

WOMAN:
Your twista, I don't miss...

OTHER MAN AND WOMAN:
But you did hit it right, in the basement, while your girl slept upstairs
But you turned me out, in the basement, while my girl slept upstairs.

The ScreamBed Chronicles

WOMAN:
I don't feel....

OTHER MAN:
Like dancing? It's a mind thang.
What u feel is the emptiness after me
The non-connection to that.... spaceman
I long to massage your wholeness, face,
thighs, booty
And U miss my tongue, slithering around
and in your cupcake....

WOMAN:
Your tongue WAS the orgasm mafia hit
squad
Touching parts of my cupcake, parts not
known
But your chance was in your lap, until your
choice
Your choice, screamed the end of our time

Brain Diary5: The future of love, massages and a room on the 6th floor

MAN:
What's on your mind, it's heavy with fear
I know that I've been busy with the sounds
and art pieces
But ur still living in my brain
My body's n pain from ur absence

WOMAN:
Well, it's like.... he....

MAN:
He?

WOMAN:
Well, my old work boyfriend, is sniffing me
Telling me things, about this about that
My heart's dim to his bull-shit-ology
He just want some....

MAN:
Pussycat...tales don't please me
Ur hiding a deeper energy within...let's talk
I'm sorry for my time bn short with u
If I could only hold u...some more
If only I could kiss ur beautiful, luscious
lips, some more

The ScreamBed Chronicles

Remember how we could gaze into each other's eyes and soul
So intensely, that we could come

WOMAN:
I miss u, your massages, your warmness, your...tongue, your penis
I miss your words, our candle incense sauna baths
Our bathtub adventure-sexing
The way u ate fruit down there and your nose massaging me...to orgasm

MAN:
All this talk, uhhmmm, got me in a position
Like meet me on floor 6, lunchtime, personal services
One at a time, glad that u wore your skirt today, uhhmmm
Haven't had u in, a few days, can't stay away from u

WOMAN:
I'll take u ALL in, my lips sealing u in
Taking u almost to the point
Then spreading my legs, skirt up high
I'll bring u into my fat, wet juiciness

WOMAN AND MAN:
In our friction town, we are the magnets
Merging into each other, we wanted to make love

Brain Diary5: The future of love, massages and a room on the 6th floor

In our short time, we must fuck
And fucking, we are
In this moment, I felt like I completely lost my mind
But it's good, it can't get any better than this....
I feel the pressure building within
From my toes, rising
My lips form a frown, like I'm crying
And.... I'm saying.... ohhhhh shittttttt

Potentials of something deeper happening from having rose petals forming a trail at the 6pm door

When she gets home, the moment is a secret
What looks like a piece of paper on the floor, is a rose petal
Then 2, then 3 and so on.... making a trail of excited mind eroticas
When she gets to the bedroom door, a note is found hanging on it
This note gives explicit directions on her next move.
She's to remove her top and socks.
Inside the bedroom, another note comes whispering at her from the dresser top
It directs her to remove her bra and skirt
(Her inside is pounding with the enthusiasm of a young girl sneaking out of her window)
She hears music, a deep slow pounding music
The rose petal trail leads her towards the bathroom
There's a note on the closed door...it says "covered skin is forbidden past this point"
She has aroma

The ScreamBed Chronicles

Removing her last piece of clothing and
opening the bathroom door,
She sees that the rose petals lead to the
bathtub...which is filled with more petals
and her serious man
She has more aroma...sliding into the warm
bubbly water
They get tender and feel each other
She explores every inch of him, and they
play lips and tongues
Scooping up his juicy love, water-soaked
floor
She has aroma, he straightens out all the
way
He opens her, placing his nose down to her
love Taking in deep cocaine breaths...she
gives more aroma
Then he French kisses her love, while he's
straight to the sky
She screams and creams
Her love sauce is parted with a whisper
They lock eyes
He's immersed in her cream of treat
They tangle on and on in the bouncing
living bed
Drenched from their merged session
(Rim shots are her thing)
Her mind and body become 1
His mind and body become 1
The 1+1 becomes 1
 (She opens her mouth, closing her eyes
tightly)

Potentials of something deeper happening from having rose petals forming a trail at the 6pm door

Then came the waters, surrounding him
He's outta his mind, he's outta his mind,
he's outta his mind!

www.ingramcontent.com/pod-product-compliance
Lightning Source LLC
LaVergne TN
LVHW091109080426
835509LV00031B/362